PEP UP YOUR WEALTH

HOW TO SAVE TAX AND
MAKE YOUR MONEY GROW

WARNING

Shares, unit trusts and investment trusts and the income from them can go down as well as up. When you seek advice, also ask about marketability. The shares, unit and investment trusts referred to in the text of this book are for illustrative purposes only and are not an invitation to deal in them. This book was completed in September 1994 and since then market conditions have changed.

The systems for selecting a portfolio of high-yielding shares or an individual high-yielding share described in the book were based on the results that would have been achieved over a period of 16 years. There is no guarantee that the systems will work in the future, as market conditions may be very different.

Neither the publisher nor the author accept any legal responsibility for the contents of the work, which is not a substitute for detailed professional advice. Readers should conduct their own investment activity through an appropriately authorised person.

PEP UP YOUR WEALTH

HOW TO SAVE TAX AND MAKE YOUR MONEY GROW

JIM SLATER

CARTOONS BY

McLACHLAN

ORION

To Helen, who has always been a long-term hold.

First published in Great Britain in 1994 by
Orion
An imprint of Orion Books Ltd
Orion House, 5 Upper St Martin's Lane, London WC2H 9EA

A CIP catalogue record for this book is available
from the British Library

ISBN 1 85797 888 9

Production: PLS
Cover Design: Orion

Printed in Great Britain by
Butler & Tanner Ltd., Frome, Somerset

CONTENTS

ACKNOWLEDGEMENTS

I would like to thank Tom Stevenson of the *Independent* for editing my work. He has also made many suggestions for improving the text and the structure of most of the chapters. His help has been invaluable.

Thanks are also due to Anthony Bailey, a former Personal Finance Editor of the *Investors Chronicle*, who now works freelance for a number of newspapers, including the *Financial Times*. He has concentrated on checking all the facts about PEPs and has also edited the text.

I am indebted to Lesley Baxter, my son Mark and my friend Peter Greaves for reading and checking the proofs and for their many suggestions, and to Chartered Accountants, Roffe Swayne, for checking the tax aspects.

I would also like to thank Eleanor Burton of the Association of Investment Trust Companies for her help and for permission to include the page from the AITC Monthly Information Service. The Association of Unit Trusts and Investment Funds Information Unit has also supplied me with some very useful information on PEPs.

Thanks are also due to Chase de Vere for allowing me to include the extracts from its PEP guide and for checking parts of the text.

I am also grateful to Mark Whittaker of stockbrokers, Hargreave Hale, for his diligent work in checking the text and for his many suggestions for its improvement. Michael Hughes of BZW was also very helpful in checking Chapter 2 and allowing me to include the extracts from the annual BZW Equity-Gilt Study.

I should also say how much I enjoyed Michael O'Higgins' innovative book, *Beating the Dow*, which gave me the idea of adapting his methods for PEPs and formed the basis of Chapter 10.

I must put on record my appreciation of Charles Fry's enthusiastic response to my ideas and for the help of Johnson Fry. In particular, David Morris and his colleagues worked on the research project long and painstakingly and he was responsible for developing some of the better ideas as we progressed. Thanks are also due to Datastream for the use of their statistical data and the graph in Chapter 3.

I would like to congratulate Edward McLachlan. I was delighted with his superb cartoons for *Investment Made Easy*, but this time he has excelled himself.

As always, I must thank my secretary Pam Hall for her invaluable help in typing draft after draft and also my daughter Clare for her help in typing some of the early chapters. Perhaps I should also take the opportunity of thanking God for word processors.

1

THE FIVE KEY ELEMENTS

I have learnt a great deal from writing books about personal finance and Stock Exchange investment. To explain complex points simply, I have had to research some specialised areas but, more importantly, I have had to think very carefully about every facet of my own approach.

To give an example, it is difficult to advise you when to sell shares. I usually manage to dispose of mine in a timely way, but I have not always been sure exactly what triggers me. Sometimes it is that shares are showing poor relative strength against the market, sometimes that the stories which first attracted me to the companies have changed, and sometimes that they have become the darlings of the market and as a consequence are overpriced. But writing about how and when to sell shares has clarified my own thoughts; I am now a more disciplined investor and, as a result, my investment performance is much improved.

Writing has also helped me make some startling discoveries about savings and investment and these insights encouraged me to write this book. I hope that by sharing my thoughts, I will help you to make a significant difference to your personal wealth.

The idea for *PEP Up Your Wealth* came to me while researching my recent books, *The Zulu Principle* and *Investment Made Easy*. For many years I have realised the strong case to be made for investing in shares; in the long term they have been far and away the best-performing financial asset. I have also come to realise the benefits of savings plans and the fact that high-yielding shares tend to beat the market. In my previous books, I recommended the use of PEPs, to free both capital gains and dividend income from any form of tax. However, I underestimated an important feature of PEPs – the compounding effect of reinvesting tax-free dividends. A statistical study by the stockbrokers, Hoare Govett, convinced me of the overwhelming advantage of doing so.

Hoare Govett has an index covering the smallest quoted UK companies – the bottom 10% in terms of market capitalisation. If in 1955 £1,000 had been invested in the average small share in its index, by the end of 1993 it would have grown to £89,000 and, in addition, would have provided an increasing flow of dividend income. However, if that dividend income had been *reinvested gross* (free of any taxes), the £89,000 would have increased nine-fold to a staggering £800,000!

Another major factor that I underestimated previously was the size of the capital sum that can be built up from the combination of the seemingly modest annual PEP entitlement with tax-free capital growth and the reinvestment of gross dividends. The compounding effect, year after year, produces far better results than you might imagine.

I know many wealthy and sophisticated people who do not bother with PEPs because the annual allowances of £9,000 seem relatively trivial. Many other investors of more modest means are put off PEPs because they think their annual £5,800 capital gains tax exemption is sufficient to cover their likely capital gains. Neither group of investors has understood the *cumulative* effect of building PEPs.

At the present level of annual allowances, a married couple can invest a total of £180,000 over ten years. With capital growth and dividends reinvested (together with a bit of luck, especially in the single company PEPs) it is not difficult to see that £180,000 growing to a very substantial sum. I already know one investor whose wife has £300, 000 in her PEP schemes and I have no doubt that in a few years' time there will be a growing number of PEP millionaires.

SAVINGS PLANS

Another key attraction of PEPs is that the *annual* allowance really encourages regular saving. As I will demonstrate later, it is vital to smooth out the peaks and troughs of stock market investment to benefit fully from the long-term superior performance of shares. Annual saving through PEPs (perhaps coupled with a monthly or quarterly savings plan) helps to achieve this objective. Averaging in this way enables investors to phase their entry into the market; in troubled times this makes for sounder sleep.

A HIGH-YIELD SYSTEM

For investors who are confident enough to select their own investments, there is an amazingly simple system of investment in high-yielding shares devised by an American investor, Michael O'Higgins, and described in detail in his excellent book, *Beating the Dow*. The O'Higgins approach was very successful in America over a period of

18½ years. I had his ideas researched for the UK market and found that, over the last 16 years, they would have produced a *significantly better total return than the market as a whole and the great majority of investment and unit trusts.*

The O'Higgins system requires minimal personal effort and very little knowledge of the stock market. It should therefore have great appeal to UK investors, especially as it should also help to reduce administrative charges.

POSSIBLE USES OF PEPS

The savings of most UK families come from surplus income that has already been taxed. When those savings are invested outside the shelter of a PEP, both capital gains and any income from dividends and interest are taxed again. PEPs help to prevent this savage attack on your wealth. Once you have paid tax on your income, PEPs enable the resultant savings (within the permitted annual allowances) to be sheltered from any further tax. Over a period, a substantial tax-free sum can be built up, which can then be used for any purpose. During their lives, most families have several major financial hurdles to overcome; PEPs can

help to answer all of them: repaying the mortgage, planning for school fees and university costs, paying for weddings and sabbaticals and, finally, supplementing pensions.

PEP mortgages are far more tax-efficient than endowment mortgages, as no tax is payable on investments within a PEP plan. In addition, they are more flexible than other interest-only mortgage repayment methods as you are not locked in for a set period – you can pay in more whenever you like and, if your PEP investments do exceptionally well, you can repay your mortgage entirely. If you use the PEP route, you must also remember to take out basic life insurance so that the loan will be repaid if you die prematurely.

A very small commission for introductions is paid on PEP mortgages compared with unit-linked and with-profits endowments and pension-linked mortgages, so do not expect commission-based advisers to be wildly enthusiastic about them.

There are a number of schemes linked to endowment policies that have been designed to help meet heavy future expenditure on such things as school fees and university costs. These schemes cannot hold a candle to PEPs, which enable savings to grow without any form of tax and are far more flexible in terms of the varying amounts that can be invested and, in some cases, other matters like choice of school.

PEPs are also a very useful way of supplementing pensions. The advantage of a personal pension plan is that you obtain tax relief on contributions but, against that, you pay tax on the annual pension payments you receive during retirement. With a PEP you do not obtain tax relief on the original investment, but you do have control of the resultant funds which can continue to compound free of tax. You can also take some of your money out of your PEP tax-free at any time or leave it all in your PEP to provide an ongoing potential flow of tax-free income. When you die, PEPs also have the edge over pensions, as the underlying PEP investments become part of your estate.

SUMMARY

Before I go into the fine details of PEPs, here are the five key elements of my argument. There is nothing particularly clever about any one of them, but taken together they provide a strong framework for a simple, safe and effective investment policy:

1. Shares have been an excellent long-term investment, far better than gilts and cash.

2. Savings plans minimise the risk of entering the market at just the wrong moment.

3. High-yielding shares tend to outperform the market as a whole. (The O'Higgins' system refines this approach and enhances returns.)

4. Gross dividends, free of any taxes, reinvested over a long period add very significantly indeed to the overall total return from stock market investment.

5. PEPs are an essential ingredient for accumulating a really significant tax-free pool of money which can be used for many different purposes.

I shall now take you through each of these statements one by one and prove their validity. As well as making you wealthier, I hope my ideas will help you to obtain greater satisfaction and enjoyment from the more active investment of your savings.

2

SHARES AS A LONG-TERM INVESTMENT

I like a man who's mature, sophisticated, suave, good looking & has invested in equities since 1919...

We all know people who have made a killing on the Stock Exchange with shares like Racal and Rentokil. According to Datastream, £1,000 invested in Racal 20 years ago would in mid-1994 be worth about £160,000, and £1,000 in Rentokil would have grown to over £60,000. In addition, investors would have received a growing and substantial stream of annual dividends.

There are many other examples of massive gains; BTR, Hanson, Glaxo and Rothmans have all been very rewarding investments over the last 20 years. But investment is not a one-way ticket and it always involves a degree of risk. Sometimes, a very enjoyable and profitable early ride can be followed by disaster when companies fail completely – Polly Peck, British & Commonwealth and Parkfield spring to mind.

I could outline the history of hundreds of individual companies, but that would be meaningless. All it would show is that some shares do better than others. The key point is that the *average* share has, in the long term, performed very well indeed.

THE BZW 75-YEAR EQUITY-GILT STUDY

Shares have produced an excellent absolute return which compares favourably with other forms of financial investment and with inflation. This is clearly demonstrated by the leading investment bank, BZW, which compiles an excellent study each year showing the performance of both UK shares and gilts since 1919, comparing the results with inflation. The key figures from their 1994 edition are shown in the table below:

REAL RETURNS OVER DIFFERENT TIME PERIODS (% P.A.)[1]

	1919–38	1939–45	1946–93	1919–93	1919–93*
Equities	11.64	5.35	6.70	7.87	8.13
Gilts	6.82	3.04	-0.11	1.99	1.88
Treasury bills	4.65	-2.69	0.69	1.41	1.84

*excluding the war years

An important point emerges from the study – equities (shares) have produced a substantially higher rate of return than fixed-interest investments in *every* period of four consecutive years or more since 1919.

The second crucial lesson to be learnt from BZW's figures is the importance of dividend income in the total return. The average dividend yield during the 75-year period was 5.1%, so that means *two-thirds* of the real return of 7.87% on equities was accounted for by dividends.

---

[1] The expression 'real returns' means that the figures have been adjusted to take account of inflation. BZW assumes that *gross* income is reinvested (i.e. the investor pays no tax and reinvests dividends).

The third conclusion I draw from the table is that the return from shares can vary widely depending on the period chosen. For example, the right-hand column shows the real return on equities was 8.13% if the war years are excluded. You can also see that from 1946 to 1993 the real return was lower at 6.7%. Against that, during the last six years the returns from equities, gilts and cash have been higher than at any time since the 1930s.

The average return varies according to the period selected. I believe that the simplest and fairest approach is to take the whole 75 years, including the war. This gives a good general idea of the return over a very long period, both the rough and the smooth of investing in equities. As you can see, the real return on equities was an excellent 7.87% per annum against 1.99% for gilts and only 1.41% for Treasury bills (cash). Ignoring inflation during the 75 years, the message is similar – the nominal return on equities is about 12% per annum, against 6% on gilts and almost 5.4% on cash. However you measure it, equities have beaten gilts and cash hands down.

Treasury bills are taken as the equivalent of cash as they are the nearest thing to a risk-free investment and can be cashed (by sale) at any time. In some years, building societies would have yielded more and in others less. In recent years, building societies have become much more competitive, and the return in mid-1994 is as much as 1.5% per annum higher than Treasury bills. Taking the higher rate would narrow the difference between cash and gilts, but equities would still lead the field by a wide margin.

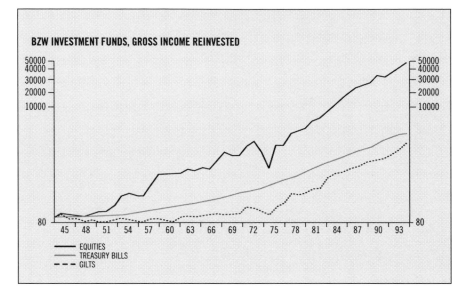

BZW INVESTMENT FUNDS, GROSS INCOME REINVESTED

EQUITIES
TREASURY BILLS
GILTS

This chart shows the same information in graphic form. It makes clear the dramatic difference in the performance of equities against gilts and Treasury bills during the 48-year period from 1945 to 1993. *There is no doubt that the average share has been an outstandingly better investment than gilts or cash.*

Of course, there is no guarantee that the past performance of shares will carry on in the future. During the years 1982–93 equities have had a wonderful run, despite the 1987 crash. In particular, the last decade has been exceptional, so there is a strong possibility that, during the next few years, shares will not fare so well. Over a very long period, returns tend to revert to the median, so a major correction of some kind may be overdue.

CONCLUSION

As the BZW study proves, shares have been a superb long-term investment. Provided you use a savings plan, or a personal system for investing regularly, you will be able to phase your entry into the stock market to reduce the risk of investing all your money at the wrong moment. When equities resume their normal upwards trend, you should then benefit from it. By using some of the investment disciplines and ideas explained in later chapters, you should also be able to improve upon the performance of the market as a whole.

3

SAVINGS PLANS

Anyone who has not yet invested in the stock market is naturally cautious about taking that first step, especially when world markets seem to be jittery. What private investors often do not realise is that most professional investors also have very little idea of whether or not the market is too high or too low. Indeed, if the majority of professional money managers are bearish (pessimistic), it means that the funds they manage are likely to contain a large percentage of cash. That money will, eventually, be reinvested in the market, driving share prices upwards. Conversely, if fund managers are all bullish (optimistic) about the market outlook, their funds will tend to be fully invested. In due course, when they decide to take profits and sell, the market will fall.

The market is contrary and perverse and impossible to understand fully. Sometimes it will go down on good news, because an event is over-anticipated; sometimes it will rise on bad news for the same reason.

BEAR MARKET INDICATORS

If you want to try to judge the state of the market, there are a few indicators that might be of help. Here, for example, are the bearish signs which often appear at the top of a bull market:

- Cash is held in low esteem. Everyone seems to be fully invested. The Americans sum up times like these with the comment 'Cash is trash.'

- Interest rates have stopped falling and may be beginning to rise.

- Value is hard to find. All known measures of valuing shares are stretched to high limits. Price-earnings ratios are astronomic, premiums to book value are substantial and dividend yields are historically very low.

- The money supply is contracting, or is about to do so.

- The consensus view of investment advisers is bullish. (You see, even the experts are bracketed together in a kind of mug index – the short answer is that *nobody really knows* which way the market is heading.)

- Shares fail to rise on good news. Excellent results are disregarded, or even cause a company's share price to fall.

- The market is a popular subject on TV, in the growing number of financial pages in newspapers and at cocktail and dinner parties. People are heard saying, 'It will be different this time.' (A golden rule to remember: 'It's never different this time.')

- New issues are chased to ridiculous heights. All kinds of rubbishy companies seize the opportunity to go public and raise money from gullible investors (including many institutions).

- There are major changes in market leadership. Growth stocks often become less popular and cyclicals become the flavour of the month.

- Unemployment has usually been falling for almost a year, making the Government sanguine about increasing taxes and interest rates.

BULL MARKET INDICATORS

Bullish signs at the bottom of a bear market are the exact opposite. For example, instead of cash being trash, cash is king. At the bottom of a bear market, most people have sold their shares believing that cash is the only worthwhile asset to own. However, once the cash they had been busy accumulating starts to be reinvested in shares, a new bull market begins.

Interest rates are usually high and about to be lowered. Value is easy to find and, based on all the main investment measures, shares are historically cheap. The money supply is usually expanding and new issues are few and far between.

THE BIG PICTURE

Whatever the state of the market at any given time, you should remember the big picture. Let us look at it again in the form of a chart showing the performance of the stock market (measured by the FT 30 Share Index) over the last 40 years:

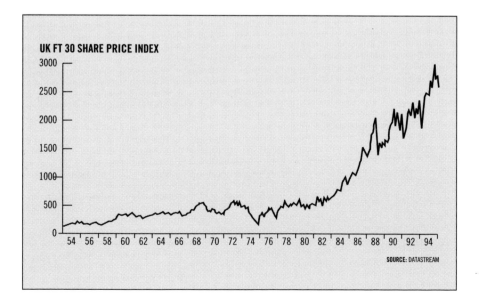

Although 1973–4 was a truly terrible bear market, lasting a horrible 136 weeks, it can now be seen in historical perspective as just a very unpleasant interruption of the general upward trend. You hear a lot about the 1987 crash, yet on the chart it is hardly noticeable. I can assure you that, for active investors, October 1987 was very noticeable indeed, but for those who had the courage to continue buying during the months following the crash, it was an undoubted opportunity.

You can also see from the chart that bear markets do not usually last very long. However, they can be vicious and a great deal of money can be lost in a very short time. The average fall in the last seven bear markets was 34%, with an average duration of about 13 months. The key lesson from the past is that it has always paid to keep buying at regular intervals, so that you average your purchase prices. If you believe that the long-term trend of the stock market is upwards then periodic falls are not something to worry about; on the contrary, they offer attractive buying opportunities.

AVERAGING AND SAVINGS PLANS

In *Investment Made Easy* I gave a striking example of how this works. If an investor had invested fully in the average UK unit trust on 1 October 1987 (before the stock market crash), five years later the units would have fallen by 5%. Micropal figures show that if the same investor had, instead, bought the units on 1 November 1987, they would be worth 40% more – a 45% difference just from buying in the wrong month. However, simply by averaging the investment in the units over only two critical months, a loss of 5% could have been avoided and turned into an average profit of 17.5% – calculated like this: $\dfrac{40 - 5\%}{2}$

The idea of averaging works well over a long period. For example, let us examine the results of investing on a quarterly basis over a hypothetical period of three tax years in a fluctuating market:

Quarter ended	Offer Price	Units bought by £100
30/6/91	50p	200
30/9/91	25p	400
31/12/91	20p	500
31/3/92	20p	500
30/6/92	20p	500
30/9/92	25p	400
31/12/92	25p	400
31/3/93	30p	333
30/6/93	35p	286
30/9/93	40p	250
31/12/93	45p	222
31/3/94	50p	200
	385p	4,191

A total of 4,191 units were bought for £1,200 at an average price of 28.6p, although during the three years the average price was 32.1p. At the end of the period, the 4,191 units were worth 50p each, giving £2,095 – a gain of £895 on the total cost of £1,200. So a profit of almost 75% was made despite the offer price being the same at the end as it was at the beginning.

Of course, pound-costing averaging only works well if the market goes up over the long term. As is evidenced by the BZW study, this has certainly been its past history. If the market were to enter a very long period of decline, pound-cost averaging would not be quite so effective.

However, it is hard to imagine shares becoming a poor investment over the very long term.

The key point in the example is that the investor continued to buy units at lower prices after the market fell sharply and during its continued weakness. There was no difficulty in doing this, because the buying was *automatic* and did not need thinking about. The averaging effect only works if buying is consistent come hell or high water. It is vitally important to keep one's nerve during a fall and welcome the opportunity to buy a larger number of units; without an occasional setback any averaging programme would fail. By having an *automatic* savings plan an investor can acquire an investment discipline that might otherwise be very difficult to learn. With a savings plan, instalments become due on specified dates and can be paid regularly by direct debit or standing order. The important point is to arrange for payment to be made in such a way that no conscious thought goes into the process, otherwise you might conclude that financial prospects appeared to be so awful that you would wait a while before investing any more money. In practice, the market is often cheapest when the outlook appears bleak. The important point about a savings plan is that it is automatic and helps you to act against your own instincts, which are likely to be wrong. A savings plan imposes discipline, making further investments an automatic process: it is a godsend to most long-term investors.

CONCLUSION

There are various ways of entering into savings plans. They can be arranged with unit trusts, investment trusts or simply applied with self-discipline to the money you manage yourself. In later chapters, I will explain in detail how you should do this; meanwhile, I hope I have established that savings plans minimise the risk of entering the market at the wrong moment and enable investors to benefit from the market's long-term upward bias and growth prospects.

4

—

HIGH-YIELDERS

You naturally hope that the public companies in which you invest will make higher profits and pay their shareholders increasing dividends. It does not always happen that way; it is quite possible for a company to make substantial losses for a couple of years or more and still pay dividends to its shareholders. The usual reason for directors deciding to maintain a dividend which is not covered by profits is to avoid the stigma of a cut in the payout. Cuts are usually bad for the share price, weaken market confidence, and impair the ability of a company to raise funds in the future. Dividends are more stable than company earnings and the dividend yield of a company is therefore an important criterion for share selection.

There are several approaches to investment analysis. Analysts vary in the emphasis they place on different investment measures, but they are all seeking to buy value at a discount. Some fund managers concentrate on shares with substantial assets, apparently worth far more than their share prices; others buy growth companies which they believe are lowly rated by the market in relation to their fast-increasing earnings; a few focus on shares with dividend yields that seem to be unusually attractive. All are legitimate approaches, but I think the reasons why high-yielding shares perform better than the market as a whole are especially compelling. However, before I tell you about them, I shall explain the exact meaning of the term 'dividend yield'.

DIVIDEND YIELD

The dividend yield of a company is determined by expressing the *gross annual dividend* as a percentage of the share price. If, for example, a company pays a 6p a share gross dividend and the shares are 100p, the dividend yield is 6%. If the price of the share subsequently rises to 200p while the dividend remains the same, the dividend yield falls to 3%. Conversely, if the share price falls to 50p, the dividend yield doubles to 12%.

The 'gross annual dividend' is determined by adding back the basic rate of income tax (currently 20% for shares) to the net dividend. So if the annual dividend were 8p a share, the gross annual dividend would be calculated like this:

$$\frac{8p \times 100}{80} = 10p \text{ (gross annual dividend)}$$

HIGH-YIELDERS' SUPERIOR PERFORMANCE

Shares with dividend yields higher than the market average do, on the evidence of past results, beat the performance of the market on a total return basis. In mid-1994 the average dividend yield of the FTA All-Share Index was just over 4%. A high-yielding share could loosely be described as one yielding about 5%. As the market average changes, so does the perception of which shares are high-yielding. For example, if the average dividend yield were to rise to 5%, I would suggest that shares yielding about 6.25% were high-yielding. As a rule of thumb, therefore, let us assume that a high-yielding share has a dividend yield about 25% above the average of the market.

You may be a little suspicious of my claim that shares like these tend to beat the market as a whole and in particular growth shares, the highly rated stars, which so often grab the headlines and appear to offer such wonderful future prospects. Three different sources have convinced me of the case for high-yielders.

UNIT TRUST PERFORMANCE

First some evidence from Micropal. During the ten years from 1984 to the end of 1993, £1,000 invested in the average UK Equity Growth unit trust with *gross dividends reinvested* would have become worth £4,257 and in the UK Equity General sector would have grown to £4,697. In contrast, £1,000 invested in Equity Income (high-yielding) unit trusts would be worth £5,693 against the market's £5,607. It is important to note that all of these figures are on an offer-to-bid basis, which is a harsh measure, as you will see later.

The *best* Equity Income unit trust would be worth a very satisfactory £7,572, with two more over £7,000 and a clutch of them well over £6,000. It is interesting that growth funds, which set out deliberately to seek capital growth (usually at the expense of a high yield), perform far worse than the market and cannot match the total return of high income funds, which appear to be less ambitious.

BEATING THE DOW

....

Further startling evidence comes from America in Michael O'Higgins' book *Beating the Dow*. He clearly demonstrates that, *with dividends reinvested*, high-yielding stocks beat the Dow Jones Industrial Average by a wide margin. He develops his theory by constructing portfolios that most years outperform the market as a whole.

To add to the safety of his portfolios O'Higgins only selects shares from the Dow, which contains 30 stocks of such a size and stature that they are almost certain to remain part of the backbone of American industry and commerce, whatever disaster befalls them. In one of O'Higgins' systems, he simply buys the ten highest-yielding of these 30 shares and, at the end of a one-year period, repeats the exercise. Any of the first batch of ten shares that are no longer high-yielding are sold off and replaced with new contenders. He assumes that both the Dow average stocks and his chosen ten highest-yielders reinvest dividends each year and his figures do not include charges for commissions.

O'Higgins' statistics prove that over the 18½ years from 1973 to 1991, an investor following this system would have enjoyed an *average annual gain* of 16.61% compared with only 10.43% on the Dow. The cumulative gain before taxation over the period was 1,750% for his high-yielding stocks against only 560% for the Dow average.

I arranged for the O'Higgins system to be researched for use in the UK over 16 years from 1978 to 1993. More on this in Chapter 10 on Self-Select PEPs, but suffice it to say now that high-yielders again performed significantly better than the market.

CAPEL-CURE MYERS PAPER

The last piece of evidence was provided by Capel-Cure Myers, in March 1991, in an excellent paper in which Michael Lenhoff examined earlier extensive research. In particular, he referred to an unpublished working paper by a Mr M. Levis, who had analysed about 4,000 UK companies between January 1955 and December 1988. His results showed that a large differential existed between the return from UK portfolios comprising low-yielding shares and those containing the highest-yielding shares. Mr Levis also demonstrated that, during the period, portfolios with an average yield 25% above the market average (our measure of a high-yielding share), as a general rule, substantially outperformed the FTA All-Share Index.

WHY HIGH-YIELDERS PERFORM BETTER

The Micropal and O'Higgins statistics and the Capel-Cure paper clearly demonstrate that during the last 20 years high-yielding shares have outperformed the market as a whole. The interesting question is why this should be so. O'Higgins offers one reason; he points out that historically *dividends have accounted for 40–50% of the total return from the Dow*. The BZW study supports this argument – over 75 years, dividends accounted for about 42% of the nominal overall 12% per annum return on UK equities and 65% of the real return. Because companies do not cut dividends lightly, they constitute the firmest part of future total returns.

A key factor in the O'Higgins and BZW statistics is that they are compiled on a gross-dividends-reinvested basis. This growing flow of cash therefore boosts the overall growth figures by a very significant percentage. The point is confirmed by more excellent statistics from Micropal. As I explained earlier, they prepared figures for me showing that, on a gross-dividend-reinvested basis, during the ten years 1984–93, £1,000 invested in the average Equity Growth unit trust would have become worth £4,257; in Equity General the same sum would have grown to £4,697 and a significantly better £5,693 in Equity Income, compared with £5,607 for the market as a whole. However, if all income had been distributed the relative returns would have been very different. Equity Growth would have been £3,233; Equity General £3,169 and Equity Income £3,219. In one stroke Equity Income would have lost its star quality and there would be little to choose between the three sectors. Of course, if you had invested in the average Equity Income unit trust you would have received much higher income over the years; but as you can see, income *reinvested* was the main difference between the performance records.

The stream of extra cash flow from above-average dividends is a vitally important factor. I wonder how many investment analysts, when assessing the worth of a share, factor into the equation the extra income that is going to be received in hard cash which can then be reinvested. In some cases it is a significant percentage which is easy to overlook. Managers of income funds are, of course, very interested in high-yielders, but managers running growth and general funds probably do not give sufficient weight to the dividend yield in their investment selection process. This appears to be evidenced by the Micropal statistics: the unit trust managers' results are much of a muchness without the benefit of a higher yield. The message to investors is obvious – buy units in trusts that regard income as important.

I believe that another reason why high-yielding shares do better than most is because they are usually out-of-favour companies. We all know that the stock market overreacts to both good and bad news, and greed often drives the prices of growth shares to dizzy heights, leaving less popular stocks languishing in the bargain basement.

Growth shares are usually valued on a number of times their earnings per share – the price-earnings ratio (PER), sometimes called the multiple. The higher the multiple the more the market believes in the company's future prospects. The average UK multiple usually ranges between 10–20 times prospective earnings according to market sentiment. An idea of the absurd ratings enjoyed by some growth stocks of the past is given in the table below. It shows the price-earnings ratios of some high flyers in 1968 and 1972 compared with the same multiples in June 1994:

MIGHTY MULTIPLES OF THE PAST

UK Company	PER July 1968	PER June 1994
Rank Organisation	46	18
General Electric	27	14
Tesco	43	12
Hanson (formerly Wiles Group)	27	16

USA Company	Dec 1972	June 1994
Polaroid	90	22
McDonalds	83	20
Baxter International	82	23
International Flavours	81	20
Automatic Data Processing	80	23

Although some of the stocks proved to be good investments, it is obvious that in 1968 in the UK and 1972 in America many of the multiples had lost touch with reality. By early 1994, most of them had shed their heady ratings.

Exactly the same phenomenon happens in reverse with shares that are out of favour. For example, no one wanted to know about ICI at the beginning of 1993, the shares yielded almost 7% and appreciated by more than 50% during the year. If a company is held in low regard, its share price falls and the shares become high-yielders. The key point is that the market frequently overreacts. John Neff, the very successful American fund manager, sums up the approach to buying these kinds of shares with the words, 'Get 'em while they're cold.'

CONCLUSION

Would you rather buy into the froth of over-anticipated growth or the despair of over-discounted difficulties? The answer is obvious. Needless to say, if you are buying individual shares you need to spread your risk and confine your investments to companies of stature that are unlikely to fail completely. If you are buying into unit or investment trusts, they spread the risk for you. More of this later; the important point to grasp now is that *on average, high-yielding stocks usually outperform the market as a whole by a significant margin.*

5

—

GROSS DIVIDENDS REINVESTED

I have already shown how important dividend income is to the total return from investing in shares. The BZW statistics make it clear that *gross* dividend income, when reinvested, accounted for two-thirds of the *real* return of 7.87% per annum on equities over the 75-year period of the study. I also mentioned in Chapter 1 the remarkable effect of reinvesting gross dividends received from an investment of £1,000 in 1955 in the average share in the bottom tenth of the market. The result is such a revelation that it is worth repeating: a £1,000 investment would have grown to £89,000 by the end of 1993 and would have also provided a growing stream of dividend income. But, if the gross dividends had been reinvested, the £89,000 would have been transformed into £800,000.

THE EFFECT OF TAX

I stress the word 'gross'. But why is the difference between net and gross so important?

The difference (in 1994) is simply the 20% tax deducted by the company before paying your dividend. Within a PEP scheme (see Chapter 6) the tax deducted at source in this way can be reclaimed from the Inland Revenue and reinvested, together with the net dividend already received in the normal way. This is in sharp contrast to the treatment of dividends received by most taxpayers. Outside the shelter of a PEP a gross dividend of 5% is worth only 4% to a basic-rate taxpayer because basic-rate tax on share dividends is 20%. To a higher-rate taxpayer, paying 40% tax, that 5% dividend falls even further to 3%.

THE RULE OF 72

The difference may not seem to be a huge amount, but the tax saving is a very significant benefit over a long period because the compounding effect of reinvesting the extra money can make such a substantial difference to an investor's overall return. There is a shortcut method (sometimes called the Rule of 72) of checking how quickly money compounds. The rule establishes approximately how long it takes for a given rate of annual growth to double your money – you simply divide the rate of growth into 72. 18% growth would therefore take about four years to double an investment, assuming that the growth was tax-free and compounded annually.

To find out how long money takes to treble, you divide the annual rate of compound growth into 115. At 18%, the investment would therefore treble in about six and a half years.

SPECIFIC EXAMPLES

To show how this works in practice, let us assume that you are investing in high-yielding stocks with 10% capital growth each year and a 5% annual dividend yield on the rising capital sum. In year one, the original £1,000 stake becomes worth £1,100 if the dividend is not reinvested. If the 5% dividend (£50) is reinvested gross, the investment becomes worth £1,150. However, a 40% taxpayer ends up with £1,130 and a basic-rate taxpayer with £1,140 (unless tax is saved by using a PEP or the dividend income is sheltered or offset in some other way).

In year two, the £1,100 (without dividends reinvested) grows to £1,210 and pays out a gross dividend of £55. If dividends are being reinvested gross, the £1,150 increases to £1,265 through capital growth of £115 and a further £57.50 is added for the gross dividends, to give a total of £1,322.50. After only two years, the investor who is reinvesting gross dividends has £1,322.50 – well in excess of the one who is drawing dividends out and only has £1,210.

The table below shows the difference over five, ten and fifteen years for a £1,000 initial investment for an investor who is not reinvesting dividends, one who is reinvesting them after paying 40% tax, another who is paying basic-rate tax and, finally, one who is using a PEP and, as a result, is paying no tax at all. In all cases, fees and capital gains tax have been ignored.

£1,000 INITIAL INVESTMENT

	Dividends not reinvested	40% taxpayer reinvests	Basic-rate taxpayer reinvests	PEP
After 5 years	1,610	1,842	1,926	2,010
After 10 years	2,593	3,393	3,708	4,044
After 15 years	4,176	6,250	7,140	8,132

After 15 years a 40% taxpayer who reinvests dividends has 30% more by investing through a PEP scheme. Actually, these figures understate the benefit of a PEP scheme because they exclude capital gains tax, which on larger sums would be substantial outside a PEP.

THE MICROPAL STATISTICS

The Micropal figures on unit trusts in the previous chapter show how crucially important it is to reinvest income. Looking at those same figures another way, £3,000 (£1,000 in each of the three main equity sectors) produced a profit over ten years ignoring dividends of £6,621 and if dividends were reinvested of £11,647.

As you know, we are most interested in Equity Income funds, which show the biggest difference – £1,000 produced a total profit of £4,693 with dividends reinvested, more than double the £2,219 if they had all been distributed.

CONCLUSION

As you will see in the next chapter, PEPs are a remarkable tax shelter. There are strict limits to the amount you can put into them each year. However, in a PEP, in addition to your annual allowance, dividends can be reinvested and the tax on them reclaimed and reinvested. The table above shows that this makes a very significant difference to results over the long term. It is the cumulative effect that is so important and so easy to underestimate. If you can afford to do so, you should obviously reinvest all dividends gross, so that they add to your PEPs and continue to compound within the scheme. *In effect, dividends reinvested increase your overall PEP allowance each year by an increasingly significant amount.*

6

—

PERSONAL EQUITY PLANS
(PEPS)

I hope that I have now established four important principles:

1. Over the last 75 years the stock market has been far and away the best investment when compared with other financial assets, such as cash and gilts.

2. Because even financial experts don't know the stock market's immediate future direction, savings plans are vital to lessen the risk of investing all of your money in the market at just the wrong moment.

3. High-yielding shares, and funds investing in them, perform better on average than the market as a whole.

4. Total returns are dramatically improved when gross dividends are reinvested.

These four ideas alone provide a simple formula for successful long-term investment. In 1986, Nigel Lawson, the then Chancellor of the Exchequer, introduced Personal Equity Plans (PEPs), which enable you to save paying any form of tax on both capital gains and income. Wonderful as it is to save tax on all capital gains, that is not the most important feature of PEPs. It is the cumulative power of being able to reinvest tax-free dividend income that makes them so attractive.

THE BENEFITS OF PEPS

There are limits to the PEP allowances, but every person over 18, who is UK resident for tax purposes, can use PEP schemes to establish a significant pool of tax-free money. You might have fantasised about what it would be like to have a secret offshore bank account and pay no taxes. PEPs give you a facility that is far superior to an offshore account. Above all, in stark contrast to an undisclosed offshore account, they are 100% legal. Also the funds in PEP schemes can be distributed to you tax-free at any time.

To take full advantage of the Government's kindness and maximise your total return, all you have to do is to make sure that you don't miss taking up your yearly allowance of PEPs; that you use a savings plan; invest in the right kind of trusts or shares and reinvest the dividend income. If you follow these simple rules, your PEP scheme should grow to a significant sum within a few years and be a source of tax-free income for the rest of your life.

THE GROUND RULES FOR PEPS

PEPs are a kind of container into which you can pack investments costing up to £9,000 every year. These must be ordinary shares in companies incorporated in any of the countries in the European Union and listed on any EU stock exchange. British shares quoted in London (including London's Unlisted Securities Market) are, of course, included and so are unit trusts and investment trusts.

There is a £6,000 limit for a general PEP. A further £3,000 can also be put into a single company PEP which, as its name suggests, can hold the shares of just one company excluding investment trusts. The £9,000 limit is for each person, so a married couple can invest a total of £18,000 every year.

Unit and investment trusts are divided into qualifying trusts and non-qualifying trusts. Some of the non-qualifying trusts are PEPable; the remainder are non-PEPable.

To qualify, a trust must be at least 50% invested in UK and EU shares and only £1,500 of the £6,000 general PEP allowance can be invested in non-qualifying trusts. Non-PEPable trusts are those with over 50% of their investments in non-qualifying stocks such as gilts and convertibles, or over 50% of their investments in shares not traded on a 'Recognised Stock Exchange'. Many of the new emerging market trusts fail this test, including Chinese funds.

Here are some of the finer points on PEPs:

1. The PEP scheme must be administered by a Registered Scheme Manager who is approved by the Inland Revenue and authorised under the Financial Services Act. Most of the managers are stockbrokers, banks, building societies, investment management groups and independent financial advisers.

2. PEPs are *usually* set up by investing cash or by transferring existing shares with a 'Bed and PEP'. You do not have to take up your full

£6,000 general PEP and £3,000 single company PEP allowances every year; you can invest less if you wish to do so.

3. Dividends earned on investments within a PEP scheme have tax deducted at source, but this tax is reclaimed. Dividends, including tax repayments, can be reinvested and, bearing in mind the compounding effect, this is strongly recommended.

4. PEPs can be transferred from one management group to another. The £6,000 general PEP has to be invested through one plan manager. The £3,000 single company PEP can, if required, be invested with a different one. In subsequent years, further PEPs can be invested with other PEP managers and earlier PEP schemes can be transferred to a new manager.

5. You are not locked into a PEP. You can draw money out at any time by notifying the PEP manager in writing, and you can terminate the PEP altogether if you wish to do so. Any money withdrawn will be tax-free.

   Bear in mind that if you take money out from a PEP scheme, you cannot put it back again, other than as part of your unused allowance for the year in question, or your allowance for future years.

6. When you die your PEP investments will cease to enjoy tax relief immediately. Your beneficiaries can keep the investments, but from the date of your death they become subject to tax in the normal way.

GENERAL PEPS

There are five main ways of investing your annual *general* PEP allowance of £6,000:

1. *Unit Trust PEPs*

These are a form of Managed PEP that offers the advantage of professional management and a wide spread of investments. Recently there has been a price war on PEP charges which has made unit trusts more competitive. Dividends can easily be reinvested (by creating new units) and savings plans are readily available.

2. *Investment Trust PEPs*

These are similar to Unit Trust PEPs and also offer professional management and a spread of risk. It is more difficult to reinvest income, but this can be arranged together with savings plans. One further problem is that the discount or premium to asset value of an investment trust is constantly fluctuating. This means that at times purchases can be made at bargain levels, and at others at excessive prices. More on this in Chapter 8.

3. *Managed PEP Schemes*

This is the most flexible type of managed scheme. Your portfolio can include just shares or a combination of shares, investment trusts and/or unit trusts. Your requirements can be clarified by a discussion with your PEP manager, and be changed by you at any time. Dividends can easily be reinvested and, in most cases, savings plans (or facilities for regular investment) are available.

4. *Self-Select PEPs*

These PEPs are managed by you. Some brokers offer advice in the form of so-called Advisory PEPs. In Self-Select schemes you are allowed to buy unit trusts, investment trusts and EU ordinary shares and you can use the £1,500 allowance for non-qualifying trusts. The investments can be all trusts or all shares, or some of each. If you want to, you can put the whole £6,000 in just one share or one trust. The investment company/broker provides the framework and the administration, but you make the final choice of investments.

5. *Corporate PEPs*

Corporate PEPs are general PEPs, with the same £6,000 annual limit, set up by large companies to encourage ownership of their shares. They are often used for employee share schemes. In most cases, corporate PEPs are administered by large banks or building societies (particularly Bradford & Bingley), have a small initial charge, a very small annual charge (normally 0.5% plus VAT) and a dealing charge in the region of 0.5%. Of the 100 companies in the FT-SE 100 Index, more than half offer corporate and single company PEPs. If you are keen on investing in one of these companies, corporate PEPs can be a cheap and effective way of doing so.

You will find the full list of companies offering corporate PEP schemes in an excellent guide published by Chase de Vere, the independent financial advisers. It also gives full details of annual, initial and dealing charges, minimum lump sum or monthly payment requirements, PEP managers, restrictions on holdings, and other vital information. To illustrate the thoroughness of Chase de Vere's guide and to show you all the key factors, a two-page extract covering a few of the companies is shown overleaf.

The *Chase de Vere PEP Guide* costs £9.95 and is essential reading for anyone interested in PEPs. In addition to full details of all the different kinds of PEP schemes, charges and the like, it also includes league tables for unit and investment trust PEPs. Chase de Vere's address is 63 Lincoln's Inn Fields, London WC2A 3BR (Tel: 0800 526 091).

You cannot switch shares from most of the corporate PEP schemes, so you are confined to investing in and staying with the shares of the sponsoring company. This is a grave disadvantage that has to be weighed up against the cheapness of the schemes. A few companies like British Airways, BET and Redland allow you to buy other shares, provided you hold a minimum number of theirs (100 BET, for example). For most people, even for employees of a company, it is wiser to use their single company PEP annual allowance of £3,000 for investing in a plan sponsored by the company in question. This would leave their general PEP allowance free for other more flexible investments.

Corporate PEPs

	PLAN NAME	INCOME OR GROWTH	ANTICIPATED YIELD	FREQUENCY OF DISTRIBUTION PAYMENTS	MINIMUM MONTHLY	MINIMUM LUMP SUM	MAXIMUM MONTHLY	MAXIMUM LUMP SUM	INITIAL PEP CHARGE	ANNUAL PEP CHARGE	HOW LEVIED	DEALING CHARGE	CHEQUE PA...
BRADFORD & BINGLEY (PEPs) LTD *PEP Plan Managers* SIB	Wellcome PLC General Company PEP	Both	Variable	½ yearly	£25	£300	£500	£6,000	£15 + VAT. Paid by Co. (+ 2.5% UT option)	0.50% + VAT. Paid by Company.	½ yearly in arrears	0.25%	BB (PEPs) Ltd Client Account
BRADFORD & BINGLEY (PEPs) LTD *PEP Plan Managers* SIB	Whitbread PLC General Company PEP	Both	Variable	½ yearly	£25	£300	£500	£6,000	£15 + VAT	0.50% + VAT	½ yearly in arrears	0.25%	BB (PEPs) Ltd Client Account
BRADFORD & BINGLEY (PEPs) LTD *PEP Plan Managers* SIB	Willis Corroon Group PLC General PEP	Both	Variable	½ yearly	£25	£300	£500	£6,000	£15 + VAT	0.50% + VAT, min. £5, max. £40	½ yearly in arrears	0.25%	BB (PEPs) Ltd Client Account
BRADFORD & BINGLEY (PEPs) LTD *PEP Plan Managers* SIB	WM Morrison Supermarkets PLC General PEP	Both	Variable	½ yearly	£25	£300	£500	£6,000	£15 + VAT. Paid by Company	0.50% + VAT. Paid by Company	½ yearly in arrears	0.25%	BB (PEPs) Ltd Client Account
BRADFORD & BINGLEY (PEPs) LTD *PEP Plan Managers* SIB	Wolseley PLC General Company PEP	Both	Variable	½ yearly	£25	£300	£500	£6,000	£15 + VAT	0.50% + VAT, min. £5, max. £40	½ yearly in arrears	0.25%	BB (PEPs) Ltd Client Account
BRADFORD & BINGLEY (PEPs) LTD *PEP Plan Managers* SIB	Wolverhampton & Dudley Breweries PLC PEP	Both	Variable	½ yearly	£25	£300	£500	£6,000	£15 + VAT	0.50% + VAT, min. £5, max. £40	½ yearly in arrears	0.25%	BB (PEPs) Ltd Client Account
BRADFORD & BINGLEY (PEPs) LTD *PEP Plan Managers* SIB	Yule Catto & Co. PLC General PEP	Both	Variable	½ yearly	£25	£300	£500	£6,000	£15 + VAT	0.50% + VAT, min. £5	½ yearly in arrears	0.25%	BB (PEPs) Ltd Client Account
BROWN SHIPLEY PEP MANAGERS LTD *PEP Plan Managers* IMRO	Corporate PEP	Both	Dependent on inv's. choice	½ yearly	Neg.	£3,000	Neg.	£6,000	None	0.75% + VAT, min. £20	½ yearly in arrears	0.50%, min. £25	Brown Shipley PEP Managers Ltd.
BUCK PATERSON INVESTMENT CONSULTANTS LTD *Independent Financial Advisers* FIMBRA	LEP Corporate PEP	Both	Variable	½ yearly	£20	£240	£500	£6,000	None	0.50% + VAT, min. £5	A in arrears	0.50% + VAT	BPICL LEP Corporate PEP
GODWINS LTD *PEP Plan Managers* IMRO	Eurotunnel General PEP	Growth	Unspecified	N/A	£100	£1,000	£500	£6,000	£10 + VAT	0.50% + VAT	½ yearly in arrears	0.25% + VAT	Godwins Ltd
GODWINS LTD *PEP Plan Managers* IMRO	Lonhro General PEP	Both	Unspecified	½ yearly	£25	No min.	£500	£6,000	None	0.50% + VAT	½ yearly in arrears	0.25% + VAT	Godwins Ltd
GODWINS LTD *PEP Plan Managers* IMRO	Portals General PEP	Both	Unspecified	½ yearly	£50	No min.	£500	£6,000	£10 + VAT	0.50% + VAT	½ yearly in arrears	0.25% + VAT	Godwins Ltd
GODWINS LTD *PEP Plan Managers* IMRO	Royal Insurance General PEP	Both	Unspecified	½ yearly	£50	£500	£500	£6,000	£10 + VAT	0.50% + VAT	½ yearly in arrears	0.25% + VAT	Godwins Ltd
GODWINS LTD *PEP Plan Managers* IMRO	Unichem General PEP	Both	Unspecified	½ yearly	£50	£500	£500	£6,000	£10 + VAT	0.50% + VAT	½ yearly in arrears	0.25% + VAT	Godwins Ltd
GODWINS LTD *PEP Plan Managers* IMRO	Unigate General PEP	Both	Unspecified	½ yearly	£50	No min.	£500	£6,000	£10 + VAT	0.50% + VAT	½ yearly in arrears	0.25% + VAT	Godwins Ltd
HALIFAX INVESTMENT SERVICES LTD *PEP Plan Managers* IMRO	Argyll Group PLC Corporate PEP	Both	Variable	½ yearly	N/A	£1,000	N/A	£6,000	£20 to £25 + VAT	0.50% + VAT	½ yearly in arrears – accrued M	0.20%	Halifax Investment Services Ltd
HALIFAX INVESTMENT SERVICES LTD *PEP Plan Managers* IMRO	BICC Group Corporate PEP	Both	Variable	½ yearly	N/A	£1,000	N/A	£6,000	None	0.50% + VAT	½ yearly in arrears – accrued M	0.20%	Halifax Investment Services Ltd
HALIFAX INVESTMENT SERVICES LTD *PEP Plan Managers* IMRO	Bowthorpe Corporate PEP	Both	Variable	½ yearly	N/A	£1,000	N/A	£6,000	None	0.50% + VAT	½ yearly in arrears – accrued M	0.20%	Halifax Investment Services Ltd
HALIFAX INVESTMENT SERVICES LTD *PEP Plan Managers* IMRO	David Brown Corporate PEP	Both	Variable	½ yearly	N/A	£1,000	N/A	£6,000	£20 to £25 + VAT	0.50% + VAT	½ yearly in arrears – accrued M	0.20%	Halifax Investment Services Ltd
HALIFAX INVESTMENT SERVICES LTD *PEP Plan Managers* IMRO	Emap Corporate PEP	Both	Variable	½ yearly	N/A	£1,000	N/A	£6,000	None	0.50% + VAT	½ yearly in arrears – accrued M	0.20%	Halifax Investment Services Ltd

EARLY ENCASHMENT CHARGE	PENALTY ON PARTIAL WITHDRAWALS	TRANSFERS IN	TRANSFERS OUT	SHARE EXCHANGE FACILITIES	TERMS FOR SHARE EXCHANGE	SHARES BOUGHT	TOP-UP FACILITIES	SERVICE	DIVIDEND COLLECTION FEE	FACILITY TO SWITCH TO ANOTHER SHARE	MEETING CHARGE
	Min £300. 0.25% + VAT, then + £10	Currently not accepted	Normal withdrawal charges	Sell same shrs to repurch. as PEP	0.25% both sides + 0.50% stamp duty	Wellcome shrs. + J Capel UK Index UT	Yes, minimum £300	½ yearly statements + ¼ yearly trading advice notes	None	None	None
	Min £300. 0.25% + VAT, then + £10	Currently not accepted	Normal withdrawal charges	Sell same shrs to repurch. as PEP	0.25% both sides + 0.50% stamp duty	Whitbread PLC shares only	Yes, minimum £300	½ yearly statements + ¼ yearly trading advice notes	None	None	None
	Min £300. 0.25% + VAT, then + £10	Currently not accepted	Normal withdrawal charges	Sell same shrs to repurch. as PEP	0.25% both sides + 0.50% stamp duty	Willis Corroon Group PLC shares only	Yes, minimum £300	½ yearly statements + ¼ yearly trading advice notes	None	None	None (£25+ VAT for proxy voting)
	Min £300. 0.25% + VAT, then + £10	Currently not accepted	Normal withdrawal charges	Yes	0.25% both sides + 0.50% stamp duty	WM Morrison shares only	Yes, minimum £300	½ yearly statements + ¼ yearly trading advice notes	None	None	None (£25 + VAT for proxy voting)
	Min £300. 0.25% + VAT, then + £10	Currently not accepted	Normal withdrawal charges	Sell same shrs to repurch. as PEP	0.25% both sides + 0.50% stamp duty	Wolseley PLC shares only	Yes, minimum £300	½ yearly statements + ¼ yearly trading advice notes	None	None	None (£25 + VAT for proxy voting)
	Min £300. 0.25% + VAT, then + £10	Currently not accepted	Normal withdrawal charges	Sell same shrs to repurch. as PEP	0.25% both sides + 0.50% stamp duty	Wolverhampton & Dudley shares only	Yes, minimum £300	½ yearly statements + ¼ yearly trading advice notes	None	None	None (£25 + VAT for proxy voting)
	Min £300. 0.25% + VAT, then + £10	Currently not accepted	Normal withdrawal charges	Yes	0.25% both sides + 0.50% stamp duty	Yule Catto & Co. PLC shares only	Yes, minimum £300	½ yearly statements + ¼ yearly trading advice notes	None	None	None
None	N/A	£10 + VAT	None	N/A		Investor's choice	Yes	½ yearly statements + valuations	None	N/A	None
£15 + VAT	No charges	£15 + VAT	None	N/A		LEP Group PLC shares only	Yes	½ yearly statements + valuations	None	N/A	None
VAT	£10 + VAT	Eurotunnel Units only	£20 + VAT	Yes	0.25% sales/purchases + stamp duty	Eurotunnel units only	Yes	½ yearly statements	None	None	None
VAT	£10 + VAT (min. £300 withdrawal)	Lonhro shares only	£20 + VAT	Yes	0.25% sales/purchases + stamp duty	Lonhro shares only	Yes	½ yearly statements	None	None	None
VAT	£10 + VAT	Portals Group shares only	£20 + VAT	Yes	0.25% sales/purchases + stamp duty	Portals Group shares only	Yes	½ yearly statements	None	None	None
VAT	£10 + VAT	Royal Insurance shares only	£20 + VAT	Yes	0.25% sales/purchases + stamp duty	Royal Insurance shares only	Yes	½ yearly statements	None	None	None
VAT	£10 + VAT	Unichem shares only	£20 + VAT	Yes	0.25% sales/purchases + stamp duty	Unichem PLC shares only	Yes	½ yearly statements	None	None	None
VAT	£10 + VAT	Unigate shares only	£20 + VAT	Yes	0.25% sales/purchases + stamp duty	Unigate shares only	Yes	½ yearly statements	None	None	None
VAT , then VAT	£20 + VAT year 1, then £15 + VAT	£20 + VAT	£20 + VAT	Yes	0.50% (min. £10) sale and repurchase	Argyll Group PLC shares only	Yes, minimum £500	½ yearly statements + valuations	None	N/A	None
VAT , then VAT	£20 + VAT year 1, then £15 + VAT	£20 + VAT	£20 + VAT	Yes	0.50% (min. £10) sale and repurchase	BICC Group shares only	Yes, minimum £500	½ yearly statements + valuations	None	N/A	None
VAT , then VAT	£20 + VAT year 1, then £15 + VAT	£20 + VAT	£20 + VAT	Yes	0.50% (min. £10) sale and repurchase	Bowthorpe shares only	Yes, minimum £500	½ yearly statements + valuations	None	N/A	None
VAT , then VAT	£20 + VAT year 1, then £15 + VAT	£20 + VAT	£20 + VAT	Yes	0.50% (min. £10) sale and repurchase	David Brown shares only	Yes, minimum £500	½ yearly statements + valuations	None	N/A	None
VAT then VAT	£20 + VAT year 1, then £15 + VAT	£20 + VAT	£20 + VAT	Yes	0.50% (min. £10) sale and repurchase	Emap shares only	Yes, minimum £500	½ yearly statements + valuations	None	N/A	None

SINGLE COMPANY PEPS

With a *single company* PEP there are two approaches – Managed and Self-Select; you can arrange for a broker or investment company to choose the share for you, or select it yourself.

With both your general and single company PEPs the *main* decision you always have to make is whether or not to manage the investments. Managing money is not as difficult as you might think but, before you make a decision, you need to know all the facts. In the next few chapters, I will explain the advantages and disadvantages of each of the four main ways of arranging general PEPs and the two ways of setting up single company PEPs. Then you will be in a position to choose the method that best suits your requirements.

CONCLUSION

There is always the risk that the Government will change the law to reduce or eliminate the tax benefit of PEPs. It is unlikely that such a move would be retrospective, so add to your PEPs while you can. If you can afford to do so, you should take up your full annual allowance (double for a married couple) of PEPs every year to save tax on both capital gains and dividends. In the longer term, there is no better way of building up a significant pool of tax-free money.

7

UNIT TRUSTS

One of the most popular PEP investments is a unit trust. I wrote about these in considerable detail in *Investment Made Easy*, but I shall give you a summary of their general characteristics before concentrating on their application to PEP schemes.

A unit trust is a pooled investment in which thousands of small savers invest their money. You can invest as little as £20 a month or with a lump sum £250. There is no ceiling on how much you can buy.

Unit trust fund managers invest the money coming into their funds in shares in British and overseas companies, gilts and corporate bonds and property. Exactly what the managers decide to buy depends on the investment criteria of the specific trust (there is a vast range on offer) and their view of the best opportunities.

Unit trusts have two main advantages over direct share investment. With the muscle of millions of pounds under their control, they are able to negotiate keen prices and competitive rates of commission. They also offer investors a share in a portfolio spread over many different companies and sectors.

Usually, the trust's units are valued every working day by dividing the number in issue into the total value of the portfolio. Each investor buys a number of units and the value of each unit changes, either up or down, every time the portfolio is revalued. The value of the underlying portfolio is constantly changing and its managers will always sell units or buy them back from you on request, because they can create or cancel units to meet demand. The better the shares in the portfolio perform, the more the units will be worth.

You will usually receive dividends from a unit trust holding (unless you arrange for them to be reinvested) twice a year, although some income funds pay out more frequently. Dividends are paid with basic-rate income tax already deducted, but non-taxpayers and PEP schemes can reclaim this from the Inland Revenue. Taxpayers have to pay capital gains tax if they exceed their annual exemption limit of £5,800. However, tax only has to be paid once, as the unit trust itself operates free of capital gains tax.

UNIT TRUST CHARGES

Not surprisingly, there is a price to pay for the advantages of size and spread offered by a unit trust. There are two types of charges paid to the management group: initial charges when you buy and an annual fee every year.

Charges vary from fund to fund, but the initial fee, or front-end load, can be as much as 5–6%. It is included in the bid/offer spread, which is the difference between the buying and selling price of the units. The offer price is the one you pay when you buy and the bid price the one you receive when you sell – usually about 5% or 6% lower. About half of this goes to your financial adviser if you use one, but you usually still pay 5% even if you buy direct from the company. Typically, out of every £100 you pay in, only £95 is invested and £5 is for charges.

Because of the bid/offer spread, if you were to buy units in the morning and sell them in the afternoon, you would receive about 6% less than you paid. In other words, before you can start to make profits, the units must rise by more than 6%. It is a costly process dealing in and out of a unit trust, so bear this in mind. For example, if you bought units when the bid (selling) and offer (buying) prices were 100p and 106p and sold when they were 127p and 133p, you would buy at 106p and sell at 127p. Your gain would, therefore, be only 21p (127p minus 106p). The performance figures of unit trusts allow for the spread between bid and offer prices, which is one of the reasons that unit trusts do not, on average, keep level with the market as a whole.

Most annual charges range between 0.75% and 1.5% and are usually deducted from dividends before they are paid out to you. In some instances they may be deducted from capital with the result that, although you may receive higher income, your capital could be eroded. Some types of funds have lower charges because they are cheaper for the management group to run. These include index-tracking funds, which simply try to match the performance of the market, gilt funds and funds of funds.

PEP CHARGES

In 1993, war broke out on PEP charges. As a result, many of the groups which sell their unit trusts as a PEP investment slashed their initial charges. Fidelity, for example, cut its initial charge to 2%, but introduced exit charges for cashing in during the first few years. Later it abolished the exit charges, but put up the initial charge to

3%. It is a fast-changing scene. Lower initial charges mean that PEP investors in unit trusts obtain a far better deal than conventional unit trust investors. Yet another reason for investing through a PEP.

Unit trust managers hope that because most PEP investors are long term, their annual management charges will justify cutting their initial charges. This is especially pertinent as they are, in most cases, continuing to pay 3% introductory commission to those independent financial advisers who act on commission as opposed to fees.

There is a variety of ways of making exit charges. For example, in just one of its funds, the Managed Income PEP, M & G makes no initial charge. But if you cash in during the first year there is an exit charge of 4.5%. This reduces to 4% in year two, 3% in year three, 2% in year four, 1% in year five and nothing thereafter.

Note that the exit charges are determined by when you invest the money, not when you open the PEP. So if you were to take out a savings plan and put in money each month, any instalments made during the last five years of the plan before you cash it in would be subject to varying levels of exit charge.

REASONS FOR BUYING UNIT TRUSTS

There are three good reasons to buy unit trusts:

1. The spread of investments is wider and safer than you could possibly obtain by buying a few shares.

2. For an individual the cost of buying and selling ordinary shares in small quantities is excessive.

3. You can invest reasonably small amounts of money, especially if you use a savings plan.

It would be nice to be able to add better performance as a fourth reason for buying unit trusts. But, regrettably, professional management has not performed as well as might have been expected. The average unit trust manager has, in fact, failed to beat the market over the last decade. Over the ten years ended December 1993, the FTA All-Share Index rose by 461%. During that period, the average of the unit trust funds under management in the comparable UK Equity Growth, UK Equity Income and UK Equity General sectors rose by 388% on the same gross-income-reinvested basis. However, it is important to understand that the Micropal figures have been prepared on an offer-to-bid basis which is the accepted measure, albeit a harsh one. The main difference arises through charges, so if you are investing in a fund without an initial charge (and with a low management charge) this is an obvious advantage.

TRACKER FUNDS

Tracker funds do no more than try to follow the performance of a share index and are usually helped in this task by low initial and annual charges. Tracker fund managers tend to trade only when a share is removed from an index and replaced by a new constituent. This saves costs as investments are not switched too frequently.

One of the best-known tracker funds is Gartmore's UK Index Fund which tracks the FTA All-Share Index, has *no initial charge* and just an average 1.9% spread between buying and selling prices. This saves investors starting off with a handicap of 5–6% (2% in the case of some PEPs). In addition, the Gartmore tracker fund's annual charge is only 0.5% per year compared with double that or more on many other tracker funds.

Other management groups offering tracker funds include Govett, James Capel, Legal & General, Norwich Union, Royal Life, Schroders and Swiss Life. An investment trust, Malvern UK Index, and a building society, Newcastle, also have tracker funds. Gartmore is one of the cheapest in terms of charges. Some of the others still make hefty initial charges and have annual management fees of 1%. With a tracker fund there will usually be a small divergence from the index it is tracking. In spite of this, Gartmore and a number of other tracker funds are usually in the top quartile of the performance rankings.

You might wonder why it is so difficult to beat the market. The most obvious reason is the initial and annual charge and there is also brokerage and stamp duty on any stock market transactions. In contrast, the index statistics are computed without any charges.

Another important reason is the efficient way in which the index is managed. Companies that perform badly (with the result that their market capitalisation falls below that of other companies outside the index) are demoted by the Review Panel which meets once a quarter. Other more successful growing companies (with higher market capitalisations) are then included. The Review Panel is therefore very effective at cutting losses and backing winners – the perfect way to manage a share portfolio.

Research conducted by the *Observer* newspaper showed that in

1993 the FT-SE 100 Index, the market's most popular measure, was 500 points higher than it would have been had it stuck with its original constituents. In other words, 25% of the 2,000 point rise since the index started life in 1984 at a base figure of 1,000 had been achieved by cutting out laggards and replacing them with winners as they entered the index. If you think about it, the outperformance is very logical and is another compelling argument in favour of index funds.

RANGE OF FUNDS

If you decide that tracker funds are a little dull and want to try to beat the market, there is a vast selection of over 1,500 unit trusts to choose from, covering 22 different categories. Some of them invest in particular parts of the world and others in particular types of investment, such as commodities or energy. Here is the complete list of categories:

UK funds
UK General
UK Equity Income
UK Growth
UK Gilt and Fixed Interest
UK Balanced
UK Smaller Companies

International funds
International Equity Income
International Growth
International Fixed Interest
International Balanced
Japan
Far East including Japan
Far East excluding Japan
Australasia
North America
Europe

Other funds
Commodity and Energy
Financial and Property
Investment Trust Units
Fund of Funds
Money Market
Convertibles

I shall come back to this list when considering how to invest in a non-qualifying trust (the £1,500 you are allowed to invest each year outside the EU). Meanwhile, for a general PEP there is a wide choice among the following categories:

UK General Funds
Over 80% of their assets are in the UK market, primarily in larger companies. They invest for income as well as growth.

UK Equity Income
Over 80% of their assets are in UK shares. They aim to provide regular and growing income with a yield at least 10% higher than the market as a whole. A very strong performer over the last 15 years.

UK Growth Funds
Over 80% of their assets are in UK equities with the main objective being capital growth. This category also includes recovery and special situation funds. The income is much lower so the yield will be below the average. The performance can be volatile.

UK Balanced
A mix of UK fixed-interest and equity investment with no more than 80% in either category. Very popular with conservative investors but, in my view, neither fish nor fowl.

UK Smaller Companies

At least 80% of their funds are invested in much smaller UK companies. The basic idea is excellent if there is sufficient evidence that the fund management is exceptionally capable.

Europe

At least 80% of their funds are invested in European securities, including the UK.

EQUITY INCOME FUNDS

Over the last ten years, the average UK Equity Income fund just beat the performance of the market as a whole on a gross-dividends-reinvested basis. This is a considerable achievement as the Micropal figures allow for both initial and annual charges and all costs, whereas the market operates free of all charges. About one third of the Equity Income funds beat the market, some by a very significant margin. I therefore believe that you have a good chance of consistently beating the performance of the market if you invest in an Equity Income fund with a good track record.

League tables showing the performance of all unit trusts are publicised periodically in magazines like the *Investors Chronicle* and regularly in *Money Management*. There are also some excellent league tables for unit trusts with PEP schemes in Chase de Vere's guide, showing the value of £1,000 invested for six months, one, two, and five years and the annualised growth rate over two, three and five years.

The performance figures exclude initial charges and are on an offer-to-offer basis. This is an important reservation because the 6% difference between the bid and offer prices (which include the 5% initial charge), compounding at say 20% per annum for five years, would reduce the performance of £1,000 invested by about £150 – 15% of the original investment.

So, how do you pick a qualifying high-income unit trust in which to invest your precious PEP allowance? As with all investments there are a number of selective criteria to be applied. The first and most obvious one is performance. How has the trust performed over the last few years? You should aim high and look for a trust with an average annual growth rate of between 15% and 20% with a high degree of consistency. This is an ambitious benchmark target figure, but you have to bear in mind that initial charges have to be deducted.

The March 1994 Chase de Vere league tables show that, for example, Eagle Star's UK High Income and Fidelity's European Income trust have both performed well over two-, three- and five-year periods. This is the kind of consistency you are seeking. I hasten to say that I am not recommending either of these unit trusts in particular; they simply illustrate the approach you should adopt. You should scour all the pages of Chase de Vere's book (or similar tables in *Money Management*) and develop a list of high-income trusts that are currently performing well and have a good track record.

Next, you want the reassurance of knowing that the income trust you have chosen comes from a stable that makes a habit of doing well. Avoid freakish performers that are the exception rather than the rule within their management group. Both Fidelity and Eagle Star have other successful trusts and clearly pass this test, as do several other major management groups.

Charges are the last criterion for selecting a unit trust. It is, of course, far more important to pick the right unit trust group and the right trust, than to worry too much about a *small* difference in charges.

As I have already explained, heavy initial charges are now under attack. Annual charges also vary – they should not exceed 1.5%. The table below shows a number of well-known groups that have PEPable high-income trusts, together with details of their initial, annual and exit charges in June 1994. (Exit charges are only applicable for *premature* exit from a PEP scheme; most groups charge nothing after five years.)

UNIT TRUSTS IN A PEP
A SELECTION OF FUND MANAGERS' CHARGES IN JUNE 1994

Initial charge*	Exit charge	Annual charge	Switching discount	Choice of trusts**	For fuller details telephone
Eagle Star 6%	nil	1.5%	5.66%	5	0242 577555
Fidelity 3%	nil	1–1.25%	nil	14	0800 414161
Gartmore 3%	nil	1.5%	no initial charge – £25 switching fee	10	0800 289336
Guinness Flight 2%	3% year 1 2% year 2 3% year 3	1–1.5% charge – £25 switching fee	no initial	8	0171-522 2129
Henderson 5.25%	nil	1–1.5%	3%	9	0171-638 5757
Newton 6%	nil	1.25–1.5%	4%	4	0500 550000
*M & G**** 5%	nil	0.75–1%	2.5%	14	0245 390390
Perpetual 5.25%	nil	1.25–1.5%	5%	6	0491 417280
Schroders 3%	nil	1–1.5%	2%	6	0800 526535
Save & Prosper 5.5%	nil	1.25–1.5%	3%	31	0800 282101

   * The initial charge is included in the bid/offer spread, which is sometimes slightly higher.
  ** This is the number of trusts you can choose from to invest in the fund manager's PEP scheme, including both qualifying and non-qualifying trusts.
*** M & G has no initial charge for its Managed Income PEP, but there are early exit penalties.

As you can see, initial charges vary widely. The 3% for Fidelity's European Income clearly has a marked edge over the 6% for Eagle Star's UK High Income. All other things between the two are reasonably equal, so Eagle Star's extra handicap of 3% would be enough to sway the balance for me in favour of Fidelity. I must, however, emphasise that I am only illustrating the way to choose a suitable high income trust by analysing one page of the Chase de Vere guide. Before you make a final decision, there are ten pages of qualifying trusts to be analysed in a similar way.

Also, bear in mind that charges change quite frequently and there are often special offers. Keep your eye open for them, but don't be tempted if the management group is a poor performer. Using the guidelines I have given, I am sure you will be able to pick a group and a unit trust within it that will be in the top ten of its kind.

Over the ten years 1984–93, Micropal figures indicate that, even after allowing for all costs, a number of Equity Income unit trusts beat the market by a wide margin. Some familiar names are missing from the top ten performers, because their Equity Income funds were not in existence ten years ago. Here is the list of the top ten during that period:

TOP EQUITY INCOME UNIT TRUSTS 1984–93
VALUE OF £1,000 INVESTED

		£
1.	N & P UK Income	7,573
2.	CDN Income & Growth	7,308
3.	James Capel Income	7,090
4.	Framlington Extra Income	6,883
5.	Gartmore UK Equity Income	6,756
6.	AXA Equity & Law Higher Income	6,584
7.	CU PPT Equity Income	6,523
8.	M & G Dividend	6,490
9.	Lazard UK Income	6,490
10.	Prolific High Income	6,419

During the ten years, on the same gross-income-reinvested basis, £1,000 invested in the market appreciated to £5,607 and the average Equity Income unit trust to £5,693 after all costs.

You can readily see that £6,000 (the annual general PEP allowance) invested in 1984 in the average of the better-performing Equity Income funds would, by the end of 1993, have become worth over £40,000. The important provisos are that gross dividends would have had to be reinvested and income and capital gains sheltered from tax by the PEP scheme. As PEPs were not in existence in 1984, the example is only hypothetical. I have given it to help you imagine having invested ten years ago in one of the better-performing Equity Income trusts within a PEP scheme. The effect would, of course, have been magnified many times if you had invested £6,000 regularly each year or even just added to your PEPs when you could afford it. Clearly, it would have been possible to build up a very significant tax-free capital sum.

OTHER QUALIFYING TRUSTS

If you are not attracted to the idea of an income trust, and prefer instead to go for growth or recovery stocks, there is nothing to stop you choosing a unit trust, or trusts, using the same selection criteria. Again look at the short-, medium- and long-term performance; what is the performance of other trusts in the management group, and are the charges excessive when compared with those of other successful groups? I believe that the income route is the safest and most reliable, but good results can be achieved by backing the right group in growth or recovery sectors.

NON-QUALIFYING TRUSTS

Up to £1,500 of the £6,000 general PEP allowance can be invested every year in PEPable non-qualifying unit or investment trusts. This gives investors the luxury of being able to indulge in personal hunches and beliefs in a tax-effective way. For example, you may feel that Japan or America offers great prospects over the next few years, or you may want some insurance against another stock market crash in the form of trusts specialising in gold shares. Wherever possible, the same kind of selective criteria should be used to identify the specific trust in which you invest. You should discuss your ideas fully with your stockbroker or financial adviser.

MONITORING PERFORMANCE

From the day you establish your general PEP and decide on the unit trust or trusts in which to invest, you need to monitor performance. You can check the price daily in the *Financial Times*, but once a week is sufficient, so you only need to buy Saturday's edition. The advantage of buying Saturday's FT is that it also has some excellent articles on family finance and the occasional personal finance supplement. An alternative is to buy the *Investors Chronicle*, either weekly or just from time to time.

However, for really detailed monitoring, *Money Management* takes a lot of beating. There are comprehensive articles on a wide range of personal finance subjects, and a detailed monthly review of the performance of unit trusts, investment trusts and insurance funds. Performance in the preceding month is shown, together with the longer-term record over ten, five, three and two years, and over the last twelve and six months. The magazine costs £4.50 monthly; for further details telephone 0181-680 3756. *Money Management* is also available in shops like W. H. Smith. You do not need to buy it every month; once a quarter should be sufficient to keep an eagle eye on your money. You will quickly see if your chosen trust is lagging or keeping up with the pack.

If the performance is poor, there is nothing to stop you changing to another management group. This should not be done lightly, however, because the costs of transferring are substantial. You immediately lose the difference between the bid and offer price, as you sell your old units at the bid price and buy into new ones at their offer price. Be a little indulgent, therefore, and only switch if the performance of your chosen trust falls well below its contemporaries.

You should also bear in mind that, if you have invested in a unit trust run by a management company with several funds, favourable terms may be available for switching to another trust within the same group. For example, Schroders offers a 2% discount, Newton 4% and Perpetual 5%.

SAVINGS PLANS

In Chapter 3, I made a case for spreading your investment in the stock market over a period. In this way, even if you enter the market just before a crash, all is not lost. In the following months you buy into the market at depressed levels and acquire more units for your money. Averages come into effect so your eventual entry price is reasonable.

Most unit trust groups have savings plans. They set up all the paperwork for you, allow you to add the occasional lump sum, if required, and let you withdraw money at any time. The minimum permissible monthly or quarterly payments vary from group to group, but usually £20 a month is sufficient to get started. Of course, to take maximum advantage of a general PEP scheme you need to invest £500 a month to reach your total annual allowance of £6,000.

Dividends can be reinvested easily, as the unit trust simply creates more units. The tax deducted from dividends is also reclaimed (with a PEP scheme) and that, too, can be reinvested to obtain the maximum cumulative tax-free benefit.

AUTIF

The Association of Unit Trusts and Investment Funds (AUTIF) launched the Unit Trust Information Service in February 1994. Anyone interested in unit trusts is invited to call a special unit trust hotline on 0181-207 1361 from 8 am to 11 pm seven days a week, or write to The Unit Trust Information Service, 65 Kingsway, London WC2 6TD. Their free starter pack includes an introductory booklet, a user's handbook and a Unit Trust Directory. In addition, it supplies a growing number of specialised fact sheets on such items as PEPs, PEP mortgages and international unit trusts.

AUTIF also has a special list of its members who deal in unit trusts, so that it can send, to anyone who asks, a selection of relevant and conveniently located independent financial advisers.

SUMMARY

1. Unit trusts are a hassle-free method of investing in the stock market without the risk of buying individual shares. They are tailor-made for PEPs because unit trusts have the facility to create new units to reinvest dividends and accommodate savings plans.

    If you want to find out more about unit trusts phone 0181-207 1361. The Unit Trust Information Service will send you on request their free starter pack and fact sheets.

2. On the basis of past performance, long-term investment in unit trusts (and the stock market) has protected capital against the ravages of inflation far better than fixed-interest securities or deposits.

3. If you want a quiet life and are happy to keep about level with the market, choose a tracker fund with no initial charges and a low annual management charge.

4. If you want to try to beat the market, Equity Income funds have done better on average than UK Growth and UK General funds over the last 20 years.

5. When choosing an Equity Income fund (or any other unit trust) there are four important steps to consider:
    1. The recent performance
    2. The long-term performance
    3. The quality of the management group and how its other trusts have performed
    4. The level of charges (not the most important consideration)
    Use the *Chase de Vere PEP Guide* or similar tables in *Money Management* to select the right unit trust with a PEP scheme.

6. Use a savings plan whenever possible to spread your point of entry into the market and reduce the risk of bad timing.

7. There are sound arguments for building a small portfolio of PEPable non-qualifying trusts with the annual £1,500 of your general PEP allowance. These could include trusts specialising in America, Japan and gold shares, for example. Further diversification into European investments could be covered through qualifying trusts.

8. Monitor the performance of your unit trust investments through magazines like *Money Management* and the *Investors Chronicle*. Switch to another trust if the management loses its touch.

8

—

INVESTMENT TRUSTS

Investment trusts are also a form of pooled investment and, like unit trusts, they are tax-efficient. Investors pay capital gains tax on any profits made by buying and selling an investment trust share, but tax is only paid once. The investment trust itself can operate free of capital gains tax, provided the managers comply with a few simple Inland Revenue regulations.

Unlike a unit trust, each investment trust is a separate quoted public company and, despite its name, not a trust in the legal sense of the word. One investment trust group might manage several different investment trust companies, but every company will have its own board of directors, who keep an eye on the managers and are answerable to shareholders. The managers make the day-to-day investment decisions.

Only a few investment trusts, such as Alliance Trust and Scottish Investment Trust, are self-managed, which means all the administration and investment decisions are taken in-house rather than by an outside management group.

Investment trust companies are quoted on the London Stock Exchange in exactly the same way as, for example, Marks & Spencer or Hanson. When you invest in an investment trust you are buying shares in a company, which gives you the right to attend annual meetings and to vote. Unlike Marks & Spencer and Hanson, the business of investment trust companies is buying and selling shares to make a profit. The fund manager decides what to buy and when to deal, subject to the objectives of the fund.

Investment trust managers look after portfolios of shares which, depending on the stated intention of the fund, may be UK and/or foreign, quoted or unquoted, and range in size from around £2m to over £1bn. The managers collect the dividends paid out by the companies in the trust's portfolio. The total of these dividends, after management expenses, forms the bulk of the profits of a conventional investment trust which, in turn, are paid out to its shareholders. Usually, dividend payments are made twice a year, but some income funds pay quarterly. The size of dividends and the degree of capital growth depend on the manager's skill and success in selecting good shares. However, some investment trusts concentrate on capital growth and provide little or no income.

If you're a willing buyer of shares, wait for a minute, I'll soon have a willing seller.

INVESTMENT TRUST MANAGER

DIFFERENCES BETWEEN INVESTMENT AND UNIT TRUSTS

Unlike a unit trust, each investment trust company has a fixed number of shares, so you can buy only if another investor is willing to sell and you can sell only when there is a willing buyer. As with any other quoted company, a market is made in the shares by one or more market-makers in the stock market. Like all quoted shares, they can go up and down for a number of reasons. The main influence on the share price is supply and demand (which is affected by market sentiment), the management's performance and reputation, and the net asset value of the trust, which, in turn, is determined by the value of the shares in the underlying portfolio. Investment trusts differ from unit trusts in a number of other important respects:

1. The managers of an investment trust have the power to borrow money in addition to that invested by shareholders. If market conditions are favourable, this can improve the performance of the portfolio.

2.   The managers are allowed to invest in unquoted as well as quoted securities.

3.   Investment trust shares can have different rights. For example, there can be two classes of share: one that has the right to all the income of the trust and another that benefits from all the capital growth. In contrast the units of unit trusts are identical, with exactly the same rights.

4.   Investment trusts are closed-ended with a fixed number of shares. This makes fund management an easier task. Unit trusts are open-ended, so their managers can suddenly face heavy withdrawals by unit-holders, forcing them to sell underlying investments at what might be an inopportune time.

5.   Because investment trusts are closed-ended the price of their shares can rise if there is more demand for the shares than supply. Conversely, if more shareholders want to sell than can be matched by buyers, the share price can fall until it finds a level that attracts buyers. The underlying asset value may change very little while the shares rise from a discount to a premium to asset value or vice versa. Unit trusts are better designed for regular savings schemes; they can simply create new units to meet demand, but investment trusts can only arrange a rights issue to create new shares, which may not be convenient or economic.

It is usually very attractive to buy an investment trust at a substantial discount to its net asset value and equally unattractive to pay a substantial premium. While the savings scheme is buying the trust shares at a discount there is no problem, but when the trust's shares rise to a premium, you will not get good value. You can choose another investment trust, but the management group may not have a suitable one to offer. This points to the advisability of choosing a trust standing at as large a discount as possible to its asset value, so that initial purchases can be made attractively. If the shares subsequently rise to a significant premium, so much the better – you can always sell them.

6. Investment trusts frequently have warrants in issue. You can, if you wish, invest in these instead of the shares, but they are riskier. With a warrant you have a better chance of making a substantial gain and, if the market turns, a greater risk of making a substantial loss. Warrants cannot be held in a PEP scheme.

7. There is no initial charge as such with investment trusts. However, when you buy and, in due course, sell the shares through a broker you will usually end up paying about 6% of your investment. This is made up of the difference between the bid and offer prices, usually around 2.5–3%, stamp duty of 0.5% and the stockbroker's commission of, say, 1.5% on each transaction. (Commission can be much higher for buyers of small parcels of shares; the minimum commission can be as much as £50 every time you deal.)

SAVINGS SCHEMES

In the early eighties, Foreign and Colonial, one of the largest investment trust groups, invented savings schemes which have been copied by other management groups. They are just like the savings plans of unit trusts: you can invest from as little as £20 a month and also make lump-sum investments as and when you wish.

With investment trust savings schemes, the managers arrange for stockbrokers to buy on behalf of their investors. Because they are buying a large number of shares, they are able to negotiate keen commission rates. All the investors have to do is fill in an application form and send off a cheque; the management company does the rest.

The main attraction of a savings scheme is obvious: it averages your purchase price over a period and minimises the risk of entering the market just before a crash. Savings schemes also provide you with an automatic discipline so that you take advantage of cheap buying opportunities even when the market outlook appears uncertain.

You may notice advertisements for investment trust savings schemes, but a more reliable method of finding out about them is to write to or telephone the Association of Investment Trust Companies (AITC), based at 16 Finsbury Circus, London EC2M 7JJ (Tel: 0171-588 5347). The AITC will send you a range of eight fact sheets explaining how investment trusts work. One of the sheets covers savings schemes and will give you the addresses of all the management groups that offer them and the names of the people to contact.

SPECIALIST TRUSTS AND GEOGRAPHICAL SPREAD

The AITC fact sheets also explain the many different classes of investment trust shares that are available and the different purposes they serve. For example, if a married couple is not using a PEP scheme and the wife has no income, with a split trust she can hold income shares without having to pay tax on the dividends. Her husband can hold the capital shares which are subject only to capital gains tax. For planning to pay school fees, zero dividend shares are very suitable, and zero and capital shares work well for retirement planning.

The fact sheets also give details of the range of specialist trusts and their geographical spread. The AITC divides trust companies into eighteen different sectors:

International: General	Far East: excluding Japan
International: Capital Growth	Japan
International: Income Growth	Europe
UK: General	Emerging Markets
UK: Capital Growth	Property
UK: Income Growth	Financial
High Income	Commodity and Energy
North America	Smaller Companies
Far East: including Japan	Venture and Development Capital

The more progressive investment trust managers are very keen to talk to potential investors on the telephone or send them information through the post. Many are now very marketing-minded, especially those which have set up savings schemes for investors to buy shares direct, and they have staff ready to talk to potential investors.

The AITC will supply you with the telephone numbers of its members – the vast majority of investment trust companies. For investors who would like to meet them and ask questions face to face, the AITC runs a regular series of roadshows around the country. A few management groups, such as Fleming, send their own staff to talk either to individuals or to clubs and groups of potential investors.

RELATIVE PERFORMANCE OF INVESTMENT AND UNIT TRUSTS

In *Investment Made Easy*, I showed a detailed table noting the comparative performance of investment and unit trusts over the ten years ended mid-1993. Investment trusts outperformed unit trusts, but the main reason was the decrease from 26.7% to 9.7% in the average discount of their share prices to their underlying net asset values. Put another way, you could have purchased on average £100-worth of their underlying investments for £73.30 in mid-1984, but by mid-1993 you would have had to pay £90.30 to buy £100-worth. The narrowing of the discount added 23% to the performance of investment trusts during the period, as their performance is measured by what happened to their share prices, not the increase or decrease in the value of their underlying portfolios.

It is obviously very attractive if you can buy into a solid, safe, conventional investment trust at a discount of 15% or more to its underlying net assets. However, the discount to net assets of most trusts is now historically narrow and, in some cases, has reversed to a premium. You therefore have to be much more careful as, if discounts widen again, future performance could be severely impaired.

Other factors to be wary of are a large number of warrants in issue and complicated capital structures. If investment performance is good, warrants will be exercised causing, in some cases, considerable dilution and a flood of extra shares on the market.

The *Investors Chronicle* summed up well the right general approach to the constant question about whether to invest in investment or unit trusts. It recommended that investors should make the most of what is on offer from the two industries; both investment and unit trusts have some star performers and a range of products designed for very specific purposes that might suit your requirements to a nicety.

HIGH-INCOME INVESTMENT TRUSTS

As this book is mainly concerned with PEPs, I will not dwell on the various options open to you for investing in the many different kinds of investment trusts. In Chapter 4, I proved that, in the past, high-income unit trusts and high-yielding shares have beaten the performance of the market as a whole. It is therefore worthwhile considering investment trusts with PEP schemes and savings schemes that regard high income as a main investment criterion. I must warn you that I am not referring to split trusts with capital and income shares, although some of them are PEPable. The high-income trusts I have in mind are conventional ones that invest in high-yielding shares and offer shareholders *both* the income and capital growth.

League tables are published periodically in the *Investors Chronicle* and regularly in *Money Management*. Chase de Vere gives performance details of investment trusts with PEP schemes, together with details of the top ten performing qualifying and non-qualifying trusts over the last three years. However, the AITC Monthly Information Service (free sample copy, then £15 a quarter for UK residents) provides the most interesting information, as it shows both the results of £100 invested in each investment trust share and the performance of the underlying net assets (a far better measure of the management's investment expertise).

In addition, the AITC monthly booklet gives full details of discounts and premiums to NAV (net asset value), gearing, geographical spread and shows which trusts offer PEPs and savings plans. It also gives details of charges, which vary considerably from a nil initial charge to a very offputting 5%, a nil annual charge to an unappealing 1.5% and a nil dealing charge to an expensive 1.65%. Charges are constantly changing, so I can only refer you to the AITC booklet and recommend that you study it carefully before investing.

31 December 1993

• UK : INCOME GROWTH •

UK specialists with at least 80% of their assets in UK equities, excluding convertibles, whose policy is to accentuate income growth.

Total Assets £m	High/Low pence	Share Price pence	NAV pence	Discount/(+Premium) %	Potential Gearing %	Cash & Fixed Interest	UK	N. America	Japan	Far East	Cont. Europe	Other	Company	SP 1yr	SP 3yr	SP 5yr	SP 10yr	NAV 1yr	NAV 3yr	NAV 5yr	NAV 10yr	5yr Div. Growth % p.a.	Gross Yield %
29	159/99	159	146	+9	100	17	76	1	0	4	1	1	CITY MERCHANTS HIGH YIELD	168.7	—	—	—	146.4	—	—	—	—	6.4
344	770/576	770	752	+2	144	32	68	0	0	0	0	0	DUNEDIN INCOME GROWTH	135.3	195.5	256.7	558.3	129.9	174.6	205.3	398.5	12.7	4.2
–	1250/960	1250	1306	4	–	0	100	0	0	0	0	0	EQUITY CONSORT (Ord)	137.4	205.5	265.3	629.1	119.1	163.9	176.9	–	10.7	4.2
127	149/112	149	137	+8	136	0	100	0	0	0	0	0	EQUITY CONSORT (Dfd)	132.3	203.0	249.0	521.5	121.7	175.7	188.6	–	14.0	4.0
–	–	735	753	2	–	0	100	0	0	0	0	0	FLEMING INCOME & CAPITAL UNIT[1]	135.0	–	–	–	133.4	–	–	–	–	4.0
388	153/124	152	159	5	102	2	89	0	0	0	9	0	INVESTORS CAPITAL	122.4	181.1	219.8	–	128.1	180.6	205.2	–	6.7	4.3
80	307/230	307	315	3	108	-2	98	0	0	2	0	2	LOWLAND	137.9	214.5	249.8	732.5	141.4	204.0	215.0	642.8	11.2	3.7
366	312/221	311	295	+5	121	12	88	0	0	0	0	0	MERCHANTS	139.9	205.9	260.3	596.8	133.1	177.0	201.6	407.8	11.4	4.4
38	149/105	149	146	+2	100	1	99	0	0	0	0	0	MORGAN GRENFELL EQUITY INCOME	144.2	–	–	–	142.6	–	–	–	–	3.8
337	386/282	383	369	+4	108	10	72	10	0	2	6	0	MURRAY INCOME	136.0	203.9	262.6	670.9	130.2	185.4	205.5	506.0	9.0	3.7
339	167/127	166	159	+4	106	2	98	0	0	0	0	0	TR CITY OF LONDON	132.2	195.1	267.1	821.0	131.3	180.1	225.7	563.1	12.6	3.7
248	399/284	394	384	+3	113	9	91	0	0	0	0	0	TEMPLE BAR	139.3	204.9	231.2	685.7	128.0	173.8	183.3	502.2	13.8	4.2
66	120/77	120	107	+12	144	2	98	0	0	0	0	0	VALUE AND INCOME	161.8	244.9	276.9	–	133.0	168.3	216.5	–	20.1	4.2
215	–	–	–	+3	117	8	89	1	0	0	1	1	ARITHMETIC AVERAGE	140.2	205.5	253.9	652.0	132.2	178.3	202.4	503.4	12.5	4.2
–	–	–	–	+3	117	10	87	2	0	0	1	0	SIZE-WEIGHTED AVERAGE	134.6	197.7	248.1	662.0	131.1	179.7	205.2	475.8	11.3	4.1

1 1 unit companies 1 zero & 1 ordinary – see Split Capital Trusts

• HIGH INCOME •

Investment trust companies which invest at least 80% of their assets in equities and convertibles which aim to achieve a yield in excess of 125% of the yield of the FTA-Actuaries All-Share Index.

Total Assets £m	High/Low pence	Share Price pence	NAV pence	Discount/(+Premium) %	Potential Gearing %	Cash & Fixed Interest	UK	N. America	Japan	Far East	Cont. Europe	Other	Company	SP 1yr	SP 3yr	SP 5yr	SP 10yr	NAV 1yr	NAV 3yr	NAV 5yr	NAV 10yr	5yr Div. Growth % p.a.	Gross Yield %
53	138/81	138	124	+11	178	0	100	0	0	0	0	0	DARTMOOR[1]	184.3	196.7	–	–	166.4	183.4	–	–	–	10.5
14	380	380	396	4	–	100	0	0	0	0	0	0	ENGLISH NATIONAL (Pfd)	156.3	184.5	215.0	659.4	129.1	159.2	175.4	442.5	7.4	5.3
37	300/178	293	321	9	113	1	99	0	0	0	0	0	ENGLISH NATIONAL (Dfd)	163.0	178.7	204.1	850.5	135.8	172.1	187.6	666.8	11.9	4.8
42	122/93	119	113	+5	100	0	100	0	0	0	0	0	FLEMING HIGH INCOME	117.0	157.7	–	–	129.2	170.9	–	–	–	4.6
31	84/61	83	81	+2	175	49	13	0	0	36	1	1	FOR & COL HIGH INCOME	141.5	–	–	–	134.3	212.7	–	–	–	4.0
35	125/87	125	115	+9	119	0	100	0	0	0	0	0	GEARED INCOME	155.8	–	–	–	165.7	–	–	–	–	7.9
35	133/105	132	128	+3	100	7	86	0	0	0	3	4	HENDERSON HIGHLAND	128.4	180.6	–	–	133.7	186.3	–	–	–	5.3
110	129/106	121	–	–	124	0	98	2	0	0	0	0	LAZARD HIGH INCOME	180.6	–	–	–	186.3	–	–	–	–	6.5
35	343/231	342	310	+10	124	10	88	2	0	0	0	0	SHIRES[2]	156.2	213.8	217.4	402.7	184.7	194.4	342.7	–	4.5	6.1
45	146/103	146	137	+7	106	35	65	0	0	0	0	0	TR HIGH INCOME	143.0	199.1	–	637.5	196.1	–	–	484.0	7.9	6.4
–	–	–	–	–	127	11	86	0	0	0	1	1	ARITHMETIC AVERAGE	149.5	187.3	212.1	492.3	183.2	185.8	183.2	484.0	6.2	6.2
–	–	–	–	–	131	12	85	2	0	0	1	1	SIZE-WEIGHTED AVERAGE	146.1	190.9	216.1	492.3	193.7	193.7	185.7	407.5	5.4	6.3

1 This company is solely geared by a debenture, linked to the RPI Index, which has a present value of £23.07m.

2 This company is partly geared by a debenture, linked to the RPI Index, which has a present value of £18.57m.

You will see from the December 1993 extract opposite details of the constituents, performance and other relevant statistics of investment trusts in the UK Income Growth and High Income sectors. To the right of the company names are the performance figures with *net* income reinvested, both for the shares and the net assets. I have highlighted below the difference between the two on £100 invested over the last ten years. As you can see, the narrowing of discounts to net assets has helped the performance of the share prices in comparison with both the market and the performance of the underlying assets:

	Arithmetic Average over 10 years	
	Share Price	NAV
	£	£
UK Income Growth	652.0	503.4*
High Income	637.0	484.0

The £503.4 and £484 figures average £493.7 and, on a *net* income reinvested basis, compare with Micropal's £489.9 for unit trusts in the Equity Income sector and £498.1 for the stock market as a whole.

However, costs now rear their ugly heads. The unit trust figures from Micropal are on an offer-to-bid basis, whereas those for investment trusts are calculated mid-market to mid-market. Both buying and selling costs and the whole of the spread has to be taken into account to compare performance fairly. In June 1994, the market price of Foreign and Colonial High Income, for example, was 62–64p. The 2p spread is 3% of the purchase price and 0.5% stamp duty must be added to this, together with, say, 1.5% for brokerage each way. The total of about 6.5% deducted from the £493.7 brings it down to

---

*The .4 is, of course, .40, i.e. 40p. I have left all the figures with one decimal place to relate them to those shown in the AITC Monthly Information Service.

£461.6 – not a large difference over ten years from the £489.9 for the average Equity Income unit trust.

These figures are, of course, all based on averages. Individual unit and investment trusts may have performed much better. You can see that, as far as high-yielding collective funds are concerned, it makes sense to consider investment trusts alongside unit trusts on an equal footing. When comparing investment trusts with each other and with unit trusts, consistent performance, the management group and charges have to be taken into account. However, to evaluate an investment trust's relative performance the AITC tables should be used, as these show the results based upon the growth in the underlying net assets. You also have to ensure that you buy into investment trusts at a discount to net asset value. As you can see from the Discount/(+ Premium) column, in December 1993 the majority of income investment trust shares stood at a premium to their net assets. This makes them much less attractive than they were at the beginning of the ten-year period.

Another vital point to remember is that if you have found a trust that has performed well over the short, medium and long term (not standing at a premium to asset value), a small difference in charges is not a serious matter. It is a factor that might sway you one way or the other only if all things are reasonably equal (a very rare state of affairs).

A final consideration is the number of warrants in issue as, when and if they are exercised, shareholders' gains will be diluted.

MONITORING PERFORMANCE

Monitoring the performance of your investment trust shares is very similar to the method used with unit trusts outlined in the previous chapter. Saturday's *Financial Times* is an easy way to check prices regularly and *Money Management* is again a valuable monthly investment tool. Again, the AITC Monthly Information Service on at least a quarterly basis is crucial as it alone gives the performance of both the underlying net assets and the share prices, together with other relevant information.

SUMMARY

1. This chapter only gives a brief outline of the complex subject of investment trusts. I have concentrated on High Income trusts and their application to PEPs. Investors interested in a full and detailed exposition of investment trusts should read *Investment Made Easy*.

2. Investment trusts are an attractive way of investing in shares and the stock market without the risk of buying individual shares. They are more flexible than unit trusts because they can borrow and invest in unquoted securities.

3. Investment trusts have a fixed number of shares in issue, so they are not embarrassed by sudden swings in investor sentiment, which can cause substantial influxes of money or major withdrawals.

4. There is a wide variety of investment trusts available to meet the differing needs of investors. Most people need the help of a professional adviser when selecting the appropriate ones to meet their personal requirements.

5. The charges of the best investment trusts are cheaper than most unit trusts. However, there are a few exceptions, like unit trust tracker funds, and there is a growing tendency for unit trusts to cut their initial charges for PEP investors. Also, the comparison of charges does not take into account the offer-to-bid spread in buying an investment trust share, brokerage and stamp duty. Once these are included, there is little to choose between the two.

6. Over the last ten years, the average High Income investment trust performed about the same as the average Equity Income unit trust after allowing for the narrowing of the investment trust discount to NAV and charges. Broadly speaking, investment and unit trusts should be considered for PEPs on an equal footing, but different selection criteria are needed.

7. The main factors to be considered when choosing a conventional investment trust share are the *long-term* performance record, the level of gearing, the discount to NAV and the number of warrants in issue. The ideal but unlikely combination is excellent performance, moderate gearing, a substantial discount to NAV and few, if any, warrants.

    When making a choice, you usually need to balance performance against the discount. The better the performance the nearer to NAV you should be prepared to pay. *Avoid buying any trust at a premium to NAV.*

8. Your general PEP annual allowance can be invested each year in qualifying investment trusts, but investment trust shares, like unit trusts, are not allowed to be held in your single company PEP. £1,500 out of your £6,000 general PEP allowance can be invested each year in non-qualifying investment trusts specialising in such territories as Japan and America. The overall performance of these trusts has been very good in recent years, reflecting the higher growth rates in these areas and increased global investor interest.

9. Warrants in investment trusts can also be purchased. They are highly geared to capital growth and, in the main, only suitable for speculators. Warrants cannot be held in PEP schemes.

10. Savings schemes are often the cheapest and simplest way of buying investment trust shares. They also offer a very effective method of averaging your costs to minimise the risk of entering the market at just the wrong moment.

11. The best way of selecting and subsequently checking on the performance of investment trust shares is to use the AITC Monthly Information Service, presently available quarterly for £15 per annum. This publication gives details of performance of the underlying NAV as well as the share price, together with key statistics such as NAV, gearing and geographical spread. In addition, the booklet gives full information on PEP charges and savings schemes.

9

SINGLE COMPANY PEPS

It takes a real man to invest in a single company PEP. Are you that man, Miss Millivant?

Most people's first choice is a general PEP but, for those who can afford the extra money and the extra risk, a single company PEP is an annual must. In addition to the general PEP allowance of £6,000 per annum in any one tax year, up to £3,000 can be invested in the shares of one company. If you change your mind about the company you have chosen, the shares can be sold and the proceeds reinvested in another company. At any time, the PEP must not hold shares in more than one company (except in very exceptional circumstances such as a demerger – for example, ICI and Zeneca).

THE GROUND RULES

Here are the main ground rules for single company PEPs:

1. A single company PEP can be taken out with the same plan manager as for a general PEP, or a different one if you prefer.

2. The cash you invest in a single company PEP has to be invested in an approved share within 42 days of receipt by the plan manager.

3. The approved shares for single company PEPs are ordinary shares incorporated in the EU and listed on any EU stock exchange, including London's Unlisted Securities Market. *Unit trusts and investment trust shares are not permitted.*

4. The dividends received within the PEP, together with the tax credit, can be allowed to accumulate, reinvested in the chosen share, or distributed to you tax-free.

5. If a share is sold within the plan, the funds received must be invested in another share within 42 days of the sale proceeds being received.

6. All subscriptions to a single company PEP must be made in cash. There are two exceptions. The first is shares received from participating in an approved profit-sharing or employee option scheme. These can be transferred into a single company PEP within 90 days of receipt. The second exception is shares received from applying for a new issue (not a rights issue). These can be transferred into a PEP within 42 days.

THE 10% RULE

Single company PEPs are mainly for people who are able to invest a total of about £30,000 or more in shares. To give a reasonable spread and reduce risk, a typical small portfolio should normally include about ten shares with approximately 10% invested in each of them. The annual allowance for a single company PEP is £3,000, so 10% of £30,000 fits the bill very nicely.

There are a few possible exceptions to the 10% rule: you might be working for a quoted public company and believe totally in its management and future prospects; you might be in a senior position in a company and be expected to own a few shares; or you might know something special about a startling invention or new product being developed by a particular company. In any of these situations, you might decide to back your own judgement and invest more than 10% of your portfolio in one share.

As you know, shares can go down as well as up and, however much you feel you know about it, no equity investment is a certainty. In the abstract, I cannot do other than suggest that you try to spread your risk and, wherever possible, take independent financial advice. However, if you do decide to invest a disproportionate amount of your net worth in a particular quoted company, there is no doubt that the right medium for this investment is a single company PEP. If your hopes for the company come to fruition, you will save a significant amount of tax.

For investors with no special knowledge or association with a particular company, the choice of a single investment is more difficult. The main aim of most people is to select a company that is a safe and secure investment with sound reasons for believing there will be rising dividends and capital growth.

For their single company PEPs, most investors select companies in the FT-SE 100 Index, in which the current minimum market capitalisation is over £1bn. Companies of this stature carry much less operating risk than their smaller brethren in the Mid 250 and SmallCap Index, so they are all relatively safe investments. There are, however, ways of ensuring that the shares you select are safer than average if safety is your main criterion.

THE TWO MAIN APPROACHES

There are several different approaches to buying a FT-SE 100 share for a single company PEP:

1. Ask your broker or other financial adviser to select one for you.

2. Choose the share yourself, with or without your broker's assistance. If you opt for a Self-Select single company PEP, you need to have an objective in mind. Among the many different approaches, the main targets of share selection would include the following:

   a. A share in a company that you know particularly well and are linked with in some way.

   b. A fast-growing share aiming for well-above-average capital growth.

   c. A safe, solid company which is a pillar of industry offering modest income, average capital growth prospects and relative safety.

   d. A share with an above-average dividend yield compared with the market as a whole. As it happens, these kinds of shares have also performed better on average than the market, so they also offer the prospect of capital growth.

It is impossible to do justice to such a complex subject by giving you a short summary of how to select a growth share or a high-yielder. If you want to learn the best way of doing this, I suggest that you read *Investment Made Easy*, and if you then want to progress to the selection of smaller growth companies, carry on with *The Zulu Principle*.

For people who are looking for a simple system of investment, I shall explain one in great detail in the next chapter. It should enable you to choose a share for your Self-Select single company PEP with a minimum of effort or understanding of the complexities of stock market investment. On the basis of results over the last 16 years, the chosen share should stand a good chance of beating the market by a wide margin.

HOW-TO GUIDE

Once you have read the next chapter, you will understand how to select a share for your single company PEP. Your first decision then will be whether you are going to choose it yourself or delegate the task to a professional manager. Either way, you should consult the *Chase de Vere PEP Guide* and carefully examine the single company section which, in the last issue, covered about thirty pages. The booklet gives all the relevant details of managers and their initial, annual and dealing charges for administering single company PEPs. Other important information includes the availability and terms of savings plans, restrictions (if any) on shares that can be held and whether or not their schemes are Managed or Self-Select.

You will usually find that the cheapest schemes are sponsored by individual companies but, in most of these cases, there is no facility to switch to another share. However, the saving on initial and annual charges could total as much as £30 plus VAT, and on dealing costs often in excess of £30 for buying alone. Transfer charges are usually about £30 so, provided you hold your chosen share for at least a year, you would be better off with a sponsored scheme, even if you subsequently decided to transfer to another scheme.

Once you have decided on a plan manager who appears to meet your requirements, simply get in touch and ask for full particulars. The plan manager will then usually make most of the running to help you make your initial investment. He will also remind you to take advantage of your single company PEP allowance every year.

SUMMARY

1. Single company PEPs are a useful addition to general PEPs for building up a substantial tax-free pool of money.

2. To invest fully in single company PEPs, it is usually advisable to have a total portfolio worth about £30,000. A £3,000 investment would then be about 10% of your investing capital, which is a sensible proportion.

3. Your main decision is whether or not to choose the shares for your single company PEPs on your own or to arrange for a professional investment manager to do it for you. The *Chase de Vere PEP Guide*

gives full details of the various options. Plans advised by third parties are more costly than if you make your own investment selections. Selecting shares yourself saves paying for investment advice and enables you to take advantage of keener terms for dealing commissions and management of single company PEPs.

4. If you opt for a Self-Select single company PEP, you can approach the problem of choosing a share in several different ways. However, you need to be sure that you fully understand the subject first. Meanwhile, as you will see in the next chapter, there is a system of investment that appears to offer an attractive way of selecting the right share for a single company PEP. *On the basis of past results*, the system has usually beaten the market by a wide margin.

10

___

SELF-SELECT PEPS

Self-Select PEPs are generally thought to be of most interest to experienced investors. I hope to show you how to benefit from them with minimal effort and very little knowledge of the stock market.

If you decide upon Self-Select PEPs, you will be responsible for choosing your own investments, which for general PEPs can be shares, unit or investment trusts or a combination of any two or three of them. You will also need to select the share to take up your single company PEP allowance each year.

You will not always be completely on your own with Self-Select PEPs. In practice, many smaller brokers will be only too pleased to discuss your investment choices and give you the benefit of their advice. Larger brokers might suggest an Advisory PEP, which is similar to Self-

Select but is specifically designed for investors who need advice. A detailed list of brokers offering this kind of service and their charges is provided in the *Chase de Vere PEP Guide*. As you would expect, the annual Advisory PEP charge is usually higher than for Self-Select and dealing commissions are often hefty. The Chase de Vere booklet also gives details of many of the brokers who offer Self-Select PEPs, together with other key information such as their charges and dealing costs.

NON-QUALIFYING TRUSTS

We have already examined unit and investment trust PEPs in some detail. There is nothing to stop you choosing a portfolio of them for your Self-Select PEP. If you want to obtain geographical spread it makes sense to take full advantage of the £1,500 annual allowance for non-qualifying trusts and use it to invest in unit or investment trusts that specialise in your chosen areas. This kind of investment can be made in tandem with a portfolio of EU shares and is the only effective way of benefiting, *in a PEP*, from the higher long-term growth rates expected in countries like Japan and America. Non-qualifying trusts also allow you to insure against world currency turmoil by investing in trusts that concentrate on gold-mining shares.

SELECTING SHARES

Now let us look at how to select the right shares for your PEPs. There are many different approaches. You can if you wish buy shares in small companies which, over the last 40 years, have on average grown 4% per annum faster than the market as a whole. However, being small they carry higher operational risk, so much more care is needed in selecting them. Another option is to buy shares in leading growth companies that satisfy a number of investment criteria, or simply to invest in companies in industries which appear to have outstanding future prospects. These kinds of approaches are reviewed and explained in great detail in my other books.

BEATING THE DOW

My aim in this chapter is to show you a method of investing that appears, *on the basis of past performance*, to be a relatively trouble-free way of selecting shares for both your general and single company PEPs each year.

In earlier chapters, I mentioned Michael O'Higgins' book *Beating the Dow*. I strongly recommend you to read this excellent paperback, which costs £8.99 and is published by Harper Collins. *Beating the Dow* is a light and easy read which fully explains the thinking behind O'Higgins' system of investment. Although you already know some of O'Higgins' ideas, I will restate his main theories briefly. It is important that you should understand his approach and how and why it works.

THE SIZE FACTOR

O'Higgins argues that the 30 American companies that constitute the Dow Jones Industrial Average (the Dow) are all of such a size and substance that *even in extreme circumstances* they are unlikely to fail completely. Manville Corporation, the world's largest producer of asbestos, was a rare exception as a result of massive law suits for fatal and debilitating lung diseases caused by asbestos. However, the tragic explosion at Union Carbide's plant in Bhopal was, for example, only a major setback to that company. For a smaller business, even after insurance cover, the hundreds of claims for loss of life alone could have been terminal.

Selecting shares that are very unlikely to fail reduces the downside risk that is ever-present with all shares and especially with smaller companies. Every year, there are a number of unexpected failures but, with almost no exceptions, not among the 30 shares in the Dow. The average performance of the market as a whole is made up of hundreds of pluses and minuses. By removing the potential major minus of complete failure, an investor is already on the way to beating the market.

BENJAMIN GRAHAM'S PARTNER

O'Higgins' second argument is that stock markets overreact. Good news and excessive hopes can propel shares to giddy heights; bad news and exaggerated fears can drive them down to bargain-basement levels.

Benjamin Graham, the legendary American investor, illustrates the vagaries of the market well. He asks you to imagine that you are in business with a neurotic partner (the market). Every day your partner names a price at which he is prepared to sell you his share of the business or buy yours.

On some mornings, your partner is feeling on top of the world and offers you a high price for your share; on others, he feels depressed and offers you a low one. Some days he might only see good news ahead and sometimes prospects for the business seem to him to be inordinately gloomy. The key point is that, except perhaps in a very minor way, the underlying value of the business does not change while he is making these wildly fluctuating offers. The obvious lesson from Graham's analogy is to seek to buy the market, or a particular group of shares within it, when most investors are depressed and the mood is downbeat. More than likely, the gloom and doom will have been overdone.

There is a simple way of identifying many of the shares that are out of favour – they are usually high-yielding. If the companies in question were in favour, their share prices would be higher and, as a consequence, their dividend yields would be lower.

High-yielding shares are often much better backed by assets. This is logical – their lower share prices are nearer to their underlying book values or even standing at a discount to them. Conversely, very popular growth shares often have astronomic price-earnings ratios, soar miles above book value and offer negligible dividend yields. Market forces work both ways. It is obviously better to try to buy shares which are lowly priced by the stock market due to exaggerated fears, rather than those that are full of the froth of excessive hopes.

DIVIDENDS

O'Higgins' third argument is that dividends are not cut lightly and form the firmest part of overall returns. This was confirmed by the BZW Equity-Gilt Study outlined in Chapter 2.

THE KEY ELEMENTS

Here then are the three key elements of O'Higgins' share selection theory:

1. The largest companies are the safest. By buying their shares you are already on the way to beating the market average, which is dragged down by the complete failure of some of its constituents.

2. Within the relatively safe larger companies, the best value is to be found in shares that are out of favour and therefore tend to have higher than average dividend yields.

3. Dividends make a very significant contribution to overall investment returns and are by far the safest part of them.

O'HIGGINS' PRINCIPAL METHODS

Over an 18½-year period ended mid-1991, O'Higgins researched several methods of investing in Dow stocks. His principal methods for choosing stocks every year were:

1. The ten Dow stocks with the highest dividend yields.

2. The five Dow stocks with the lowest share prices selected from the ten with the highest dividend yields.

3. The stock with the second-lowest share price, selected from the ten highest-yielders in the Dow. O'Higgins calls this the 'Penultimate Profit Prospect'.

The *total returns* (capital growth plus dividends) from the three methods over 18½ years are shown in the table below:

		Average Annual Total Return %	Cumulative Total Return %
1.	Ten highest-yielders	16.61	1,753
2.	Five high-yield/lowest-priced stocks	19.43	2,819
3.	Penultimate Profit Prospect	24.41	6,245

In comparison with these startling performances, the average annual total return on the Dow over the 18½-year period was 10.43% giving a cumulative total return of only 559%.

In America, the five highest-yielders with the lowest share prices beat the Dow 15 years out of 18½. On average, half the stocks had to be replaced each year. Costs are not included in O'Higgins' figures and, as shares were selected once a year over the 18½ years, there would have been a sizeable turnover. With the portfolio of ten highest-yielders about a third of the stocks were replaced each year. O'Higgins recommends using an execution-only broker and estimates that total dealing costs would have reduced the overall return by 3% per annum. However, even after making this allowance, the relative performance of his system is stunning.

Now let us go back to see exactly how O'Higgins achieves these spectacular results. First the high-yield system – once a year he simply selects the ten highest-yielding stocks from the 30 in the Dow. At the end of each year he repeats the whole exercise, keeping the stocks that are still among the highest-yielders and replacing those that no longer qualify with new candidates.

With the high-yield/lowest-priced system, O'Higgins selects the five shares with the lowest share prices from the ten highest-yielders. Again, this is a yearly process.

O'Higgins' reason for selecting the shares with the lowest prices is that they tend to have lower market capitalisations and are usually subject to larger percentage changes. I was surprised that he used the share price rather than the market capitalisation as a criterion, but in America the two are more closely related than in the UK. Here, for reasons of marketability, high share prices are often reduced by way of scrip issues of new shares. In America, there is a much wider variance between the highest and lowest share prices in leading stocks, while in the UK there is greater convergence especially in the 250–500p range.

O'Higgins' third system, his so-called Penultimate Profit Prospect, is simply the share out of the ten highest-yielders with the second-lowest share price. As you can see, this performed for him best of all.

O'HIGGINS' SYSTEM IN THE UK

The *Financial Times* tested the O'Higgins system in the UK, selecting the lowest-priced shares of the ten highest-yielders from the FT 30 Share Index. During the period 1979–92 it found that £10,000, *with gross dividends reinvested*, grew to £130,000 against £81,540 for the same sum invested in the FTA All-Share Index.

Fascinated by O'Higgins' approach, I decided to research his system further in the UK. In particular, I wanted to see if his idea of the Penultimate Profit Prospect worked here and if lowest market capitalisation would be a better measure than lowest share price for the final selection of five shares from the ten highest-yielders. I was also interested to see how high-yielders work on their own and how the results compare with low-yielders.

In addition to answering these questions I wanted to make the system both accessible and user-friendly to the small PEP investor. For that reason I decided to begin with the top 30 UK companies measured by market capitalisation each year. These companies are listed in most of the Sunday papers so they are easy to find. Also their shares can be traded in volume and are amongst the safest and most secure in the UK.

With these thoughts in mind, I approached Charles Fry of Johnson Fry, the innovative investment specialists, and asked if he would be interested in working with me to research the O'Higgins principle and its application to the UK market. He was fascinated by the idea and could readily see how attractive it might be to small investors, especially for PEP schemes.

With the help of Datastream, Johnson Fry did a masterly job for me. Its sources and methods (in particular, the assumptions made for calculating total returns) are set out in the Appendix. The key results are shown overleaf.

TEN HIGHEST-YIELDERS

As you can see, the compound rate of total return of the FTA All-Share Index during the ten-year period ended December 1993 was a surprisingly high 18.8% per annum. This is a very good performance that is difficult to beat consistently. However, the ten highest-yielders gave a compound annual total return of 22.4%. As you know, 3.6% extra is a significant difference on a cumulative basis. In the ten years ended 1993, it made its mark – the cumulative return was 656.6% against 459.1% for the FTA All-Share Index.

Johnson Fry also tested the ten lowest-yielders (mainly growth stocks) to find that their performance of 17.7% per annum compound was below average by 1.1%. It was important to check how they fared to see the other side of the coin.

As you can see from the year-by-year detailed figures, the ten highest-yielders beat the index of the top 30 shares in the FT-SE 100 in six years out of ten. In their two worst years they underperformed the other 30 shares by 10.1% (21.4% against 31.5%) and 5.3% (-12.1% against -6.8%). In their three best years, they were better by over 20% (38.3% against 18.2%), 15% and 13%.

It is also vital to contrast the performance of the high-yielders

SUMMARY OF ANNUAL RETURNS FOR PORTFOLIOS DEVELOPED FROM THE FT-SE 100 TOP 30 COMPANIES BY MARKET VALUE FOR THE TEN-YEAR PERIOD 1984–93

YEAR ENDING 31st December	All-share %	Top 30 %	10 Highest Yielders of Top 30 %	10 Lowest Yielders of Top 30 %	Highest Yielder of Top 30 %	Second Highest Yielder of Top 30 %	Second Lowest Priced of 10 Highest Yielders %	5 Lowest Priced of 10 Highest Yielders %	5 Lowest Mkt Value of 10 Highest Yielders %
1984	32.0	28.6	36.9	35.8	29.2	32.8	103.2	47.0	32.4
1985	20.1	16.3	28.9	5.7	24.2	51.8	30.4	43.0	38.8
1986	27.5	26.6	41.5	19.0	38.9	56.2	52.4	40.1	41.5
1987	8.0	7.3	5.6	10.2	11.1	14.9	3.3	4.8	0.4
1988	11.5	8.4	5.1	3.8	5.7	12.0	21.5	8.4	3.4
1989	36.1	45.9	47.3	50.8	15.3	48.7	62.4	46.5	42.3
1990	-9.7	-6.8	-12.1	-6.7	-17.2	5.1	-19.3	-8.3	-16.7
1991	20.7	31.5	21.4	47.3	12.5	48.2	16.0	22.3	22.8
1992	20.5	24.2	25.6	17.9	54.5	-10.4	48.2	34.3	26.4
1993	28.4	18.2	38.3	6.7	70.8	60.1	49.3	38.1	47.4
COMPOUND ANNUAL RETURN	18.8	19.2	22.4	17.7	22.2	29.7	32.8	26.1	22.0
AVERAGE ANNUAL RETURN	19.5	20.0	23.8	19.0	24.5	31.9	36.8	27.6	23.9

against the FTA All-Share Index. They win seven times and lose three. The worst performance is only 6.4% less than the market, whereas the best are about 14%, 11% and 10% better. It is pertinent to note that on average only 30% of the portfolio needed replacing each year and out of the extra 3.6% of better compound annual return, about half of it was accounted for by higher dividend yields.

FIVE LOWEST-PRICED/HIGHEST-YIELDERS

Now let us look at the five lowest-priced of the top ten highest-yielding companies. Here the results are a more impressive 26.1% compound over the ten-year period – 7.3% better than the FTA All-Share Index. The cumulative total return (without taking costs into account) was more than double at 918.7% against 459.1% for the market as a whole.

The results are also more consistent. The O'Higgins system wins in eight years out of ten against the FTA All-Share Index and in six years (with one tie) against the top 30 companies. The worst performance against the FTA All-Share Index is 3.2% less (4.8% against 8.0%). In contrast, there are five years of outperformance of more than 10% including one year of 15.0% and another of 22.9%

I was surprised to find that using lower market capitalisations instead of lower prices for selecting the final five shares did not have a better outcome. The compound annual return of 22.0% was, however, still 3.2% better than the FTA All-Share Index. Good, but nowhere near the 7.3% per annum improvement from O'Higgins' basic lowest-price approach.

THE 'PENULTIMATE PROFIT PROSPECT'

O'Higgins' idea of selecting the second lowest-priced share of the ten highest-yielders in the top 30 companies also worked well in the

UK. The system beat the market by a massive 14% producing a compound annual total rate of return of 32.8%. However, a major contribution to the profits came from the 103.2% gain in 1984. A ten-year test taken in 1995 might therefore produce a much less favourable outcome.

Johnson Fry also researched for me the results of simply selecting the second highest-yielder from the top 30 shares. The 29.7% compound annual return is a very satisfactory 10.9% better than the market. It is also more consistent and does not rely on one exceptional gain. I therefore prefer the second highest-yielder (as opposed to the second lowest-priced of the ten highest-yielders) as the way of selecting a high-yielding share for a single company PEP.

What kind of UK companies have beaten the market nine years out of ten and produced a compound annual return of 29.7% over the last ten years? Here is the list:

THE SECOND HIGHEST-YIELDERS OF TOP 30 COMPANIES

Year	Company	Total Return %	FTA All-Share Total Return %	Gain or Loss against FTA All-Share %
1984	Imperial Group	32.8	32.0	0.8
1985	Imperial Group	51.8	20.1	31.7
1986	Shell Transport	56.2	27.5	28.7
1987	British Gas	14.9	8.0	6.9
1988	Barclays	12.0	11.5	0.5
1989	Barclays	48.7	36.1	12.6
1990	British Petroleum	5.1	-9.7	14.8
1991	ICI	48.2	20.7	27.5
1992	British Petroleum	-10.4	20.5	-30.9
1993	ICI	60.1	28.4	31.7
Average Annual Return		31.9	19.5	12.4
Compound Annual Rate		29.7	18.8	10.9

Johnson Fry also checked the individual results for the top four of the highest-yielders in the leading 30 companies. The second highest is clearly the star of the show:

THE FOUR HIGHEST-YIELDERS OF THE TOP 30 COMPANIES

Share from top 30 companies 1984–93	Total Return %	FTA All-Share Total Return %	Gain or Loss against FTA All-Share %
Highest-yielder	22.2	18.8	3.4
Second highest	29.7	18.8	10.9
Third highest	15.6	18.8	-3.2
Fourth highest	21.6	18.8	2.8

There is some logic to support the proposition that the second highest-yielder should produce better results than the highest. The highest-yielding company could be a real dog, whereas the second highest has a better chance of being a company that is simply unpopular at the time. Certainly, O'Higgins is in no doubt that, with the Dow stocks, the lowest-priced high-yielder has tended to be a company in financial difficulty, whereas the penultimate one was usually a company that was out of favour due to other circumstances such as lower earnings.

SPECIMEN PORTFOLIOS

As you can see from the table of figures, 1992 and 1993 were good years for the O'Higgins approach, so let us look at the two portfolios that would have been selected in those years using the five lowest-priced of the ten highest-yielders:

1992

	Yield %
General Electric	6.17
Hanson	7.33
Prudential	5.75
British Gas	6.54
National Westminster	8.42
Average	6.84

1993

Hanson	6.51
British Petroleum	5.63
British Gas	6.13
Prudential	5.05
Barclays	7.39
Average	6.14

Source: DATASTREAM

In early 1992, General Electric was thought to be rather a dull company; its shares rose 42% during the year. Banks were out of favour too, providing the base for National Westminster shares to rise by 46% by the end of the year.

In early 1993, British Petroleum was thought to be in trouble with high gearing and major management problems. During the year its shares rose 45% and today a remarkable transformation seems to have taken place. Barclays, too, was having its problems at the beginning of 1993 but during the year its shares appreciated by a spectacular 67%.

The other shares in the portfolios acquitted themselves quite well, with British Gas as the main laggard with a 10% rise in 1992 followed by over 17% in the following year. During this time most of the companies were also paying out higher than average dividends.

As you can see, the quality of the shares selected is very high indeed; they are the bluest of blue chips. There is also a reasonable spread of investment. In June 1994, each company is capitalised at over £5bn, so they are all easy to deal in and relatively safe and secure.

FURTHER RESEARCH BY JOHNSON FRY

Intrigued by the results of our preliminary research, I asked Johnson Fry to go back further to see how the O'Higgins principle would have worked over a longer period. The FT-SE 100 Share Index was only available in 1983, so this made the task more difficult. However, there was an easy answer which also solved another problem.

Johnson Fry had been concerned that the top 30 UK companies did not provide sufficient diversification. For example, one of the yearly portfolios contained two leading banks and was not far from including an insurance company. If all goes well (as it did in this instance), there is no problem, but if banks experience major difficulties, the portfolio's performance could be disastrous.

The simple answer was to follow the same lines as the *Financial Times*' earlier research and use instead the FT 30 Share Index. About half of the constituents come from the top 30 (including only one bank) and the balance from a wider spread of other companies in the FT-SE 100 Index. They have capitalisations ranging as low as £1.5bn compared with about £5bn for the smaller companies in the top 30.

There is no doubt that the FT 30 Share Index provides better diversification as that is the main aim of the Review Panel which meets once a quarter to review its constituents. The 30 stocks in the Dow used by O'Higgins in America are very comparable to the companies in the FT 30 Share Index. They have a strong industrial bias and although they include many large companies, size is not the only selection criterion.

Johnson Fry again used Datastream for their additional research and made the same assumptions about dividends when calculating overall return. The results were illuminating. Over the 20-year period, 1973–93, the market enjoyed a very high average annual return of 23.7% because in the first year share prices were exceptionally low. However, the average annual return on the five lowest priced of the ten highest-yielders was a very satisfactory 10.7% better at 34.4%. It was pleasing to see the O'Higgins approach confirmed by research over such a long period.

Johnson Fry's extra research also enabled comparisons to be made between the top 30 companies and the FT 30 Share Index as the source for selecting the ten highest-yielders. Over the ten years, 1984–93, the results favoured the FT 30 Share Index by about 3.0%:

	Compound Annual Total Returns 1984–93		
	FTA All Share %	FT 30 Share Index %	Top 30 %
Ten highest-yielders	18.8	25.4	22.4
Five lowest-priced of ten highest-yielders	18.8	28.7	26.1

Johnson Fry was also worried that there might be a large divergence between the results achieved by making initial investments in different months of the year. It therefore tested four quarter-end points of entry throughout the year over a 16-year period. The results are shown overleaf. As you can see, the system substantially beat the market whatever the point of entry. Out of the four periods

ANNUAL TOTAL RETURN ON FIVE LOWEST-PRICED SHARES FROM THE TEN HIGHEST-YIELDERS IN THE FT 30 INDEX 1978–93

	MARCH			JUNE			SEPTEMBER			DECEMBER		
	5 Lowest Priced of 10 Highest Yield %	*All-Share* %	*GAIN OR LOSS* %	*5 Lowest Priced of 10 Highest Yield* %	*All-Share* %	*GAIN OR LOSS* %	*5 Lowest Priced of 10 Highest Yield* %	*All-Share* %	*GAIN OR LOSS* %	*5 Lowest Priced of 10 Highest Yield* %	*All-Share* %	*GAIN OR LOSS* %
1978	2.93	22.8	6.5	24.9	16.7	8.2	2.9	7.4	-4.5	1.9	8.5	-6.6
1979	23.7	37.1	-13.4	12.2	24.2	-12.0	-3.4	17.9	-21.3	-0.7	10.5	-11.2
1980	0.3	-4.1	4.4	10.1	16.0	-5.9	11.0	21.6	-10.6	33.6	35.4	-1.8
1981	35.6	37.2	-1.6	26.7	26.3	0.4	-8.4	1.7	-10.1	15.6	13.8	1.8
1982	31.3	11.8	19.5	21.2	6.8	14.4	45.8	37.8	8.0	49.5	29.2	20.3
1983	25.3	33.3	-8.0	13.8	49.8	-36.0	28.0	29.4	-1.4	62.2	29.2	33.0
1984	42.6	33.3	9.3	36.4	11.3	25.1	64.5	26.0	38.5	45.3	32.0	13.3
1985	37.4	23.3	14.1	45.9	28.1	17.8	65.5	22.6	42.9	44.3	20.1	24.2
1986	92.3	36.6	55.7	85.2	42.6	42.6	27.6	27.7	-0.1	28.9	27.5	1.4
1987	20.9	28.7	-7.8	39.5	46.9	-7.4	68.3	63.0	5.3	14.2	8.0	6.2
1988	-1.3	-6.8	5.5	-13.9	-13.1	-0.8	-14.4	-18.2	3.8	20.6	11.5	9.1
1989	38.6	25.5	13.1	40.9	19.9	21.0	46.5	29.3	17.2	52.8	36.1	16.7
1990	25.1	8.8	16.3	18.9	11.6	7.3	-1.6	-13.3	11.7	-2.1	-9.7	7.6
1991	19.2	12.5	6.7	2.5	4.3	-1.8	40.4	38.4	2.0	24.5	20.7	3.8
1992	12.8	3.3	9.5	5.3	10.1	-4.8	7.5	-0.1	7.6	25.7	20.5	5.2
1993	55.7	26.2	29.5	54.6	23.1	31.5	75.7	30.3	45.4	43.3	28.4	14.9
AVERAGE ANNUAL RETURN	30.6	20.6	10.0	26.5	20.3	6.2	28.5	20.1	8.4	28.7	20.1	8.6

111

in each of 16 years (a total of 64), there were 20 times when the system did not match the market and 44 times when it worked better.

The worst initial results were shown by the September point of entry with four successive losses in 1978, 1979, 1980 and 1981. However, even after that disastrous start, the system caught up and finally achieved a very satisfactory overall result. This further emphasises that anyone following this kind of system should adopt a long-term approach and, whenever possible, try to phase their entry into the market as much as possible.

Johnson Fry also checked the results that would have been obtained from the second highest-yielder out of the FT 30 Index over the ten-year period 1984–93. The resultant compound annual rate of return of 27.1% beat the market by 8.3% and compared with a gain of 29.7% from the second highest-yielder of the top 30 shares. An excellent result confirming the general validity of the high-yield approach.

CAVEATS

Johnson Fry produced many more statistics for me, but I have tried to summarise them rather than risk confusing the issue. The overall message is very clear – the basic five-share O'Higgins system would have worked in the UK over the last two decades.

The important point arising from the Johnson Fry research is the consistency of the outperformance. There were far more winning than losing years and the worst year's performance was far from a catastrophe. Johnson Fry also demonstrated that it does not really matter if you use the FT 30 Share Index or the top 30 companies as the base for selecting your ten highest-yielders. Either way the five lowest-priced and the second highest-yielder would have beaten the market by a wide margin.

However, the Johnson Fry research for the top 30 shares over only ten years does not prove that the same kind of performance can be achieved in the future. *Shares can go down as well as up and there is a strong possibility that there might be several years in succession when the system will not work.* There is also a chance of one of the top 30 companies or a share in the FT 30 Share Index failing completely or suffering such a major setback that it materially affects performance. With a five- or ten-share portfolio, an event like this would have a dramatic impact; with only one share it would be disastrous.

SAVING MANAGEMENT CHARGES

A great attraction of the O'Higgins approach is that you can select the five shares yourself and save some of the onerous charges you would otherwise have to pay to a unit or investment trust group or an Advisory PEP manager. An execution-only broker could do everything for you. Sharelink, for example, makes no initial charge and only charges 0.75% plus VAT per annum for its PEP management fee on the first £50,000, 0.25% on the next £50,000 and 0.15% on the excess of the portfolio value over £100,000. Its dealing costs would be 1.5% up to £2,500 a transaction, with a minimum charge of £20 and a maximum of £37.50. As your PEP grows, dealing charges will therefore come down sharply. Bear in mind that Sharelink's charges compare with initial charges of 5–6% on most unit trusts plus annual management fees of about 1.5%.

On past performance, about half of the five-share O'Higgins portfolio needs to be replaced each year. On this basis, let us analyse in more detail the likely annual charges for £6,000 invested in a general PEP, and £50,000 in a mature PEP scheme. The charges using Sharelink would be as follows:

	£6,000	£9,000	£50,000
	£	£	£
*Brokerage on annual purchase of 2.5 shares	50.00	67.50	93.25
Stamp duty at 0.5%	15.00	22.50	125.00
Brokerage on annual sale of 2.5 shares	50.00	67.50	93.75
PEP management fee of 0.75% + VAT	53.00	80.00	440.00
	168.00	237.50	752.00
**1.5% average difference between bid and offer price on 2.5 leading shares	90.00	135.00	750.00
Average annual cost	258.00	372.50	1,502.00
Average annual cost %	4.3%	4.1%	3.0%

*The £6,000 portfolio's shares would be purchased for Sharelink's minimum brokerage charge of £20 per transaction, the £9,000 one would pay 1.5% and the £50,000 one the maximum charge of £37.50 per transaction.

**Although not an operating cost as such, it is necessary to take into account the market-makers' spread on shares as this adds to overall costs. The resultant percentage figures are then more readily comparable with the results achieved by unit trusts.

The above charges do not take into account buying the initial portfolio of five shares and the eventual sale of all of the shares. During a ten-year period these extra charges would add about 0.3% to the average annual cost. Another factor to be taken into account is broker's commission on the reinvestment of dividends. However, this is easily dealt with by accumulating the dividends and adding them to the following year's investment. This adds 0.1%[1] to the annual costs of the £9,000 portfolio. The total average annual costs for the three

---

[1] The extra charge of 0.1% only applies to the £9,000 portfolio. By adding the dividends (and tax credits) to next year's investment, commissions on the resultant purchases for the £6,000 portfolio would be covered by Sharelink's minimum charges. Similarly, investments for the £50,000 portfolio would be covered by its maximum charges.

portfolios are therefore 4.6% for £6,000, 4.5% for £9,000 and 3.3% for £50,000.

The 4.6% annual charge for a general PEP of £6,000 is only a little less than the initial charges of most of the popular unit trusts. However, as the value of the PEP portfolio rises, the Self-Select percentage charge drops to a much more attractive level.

The O'Higgins five-share portfolio beat the market by 7.3% over the ten years 1984–93. The average Equity Income trust on an offer-to-bid basis and after all expenses, just beat the market over the same period. Bearing in mind the extra hassle, the 4.7% annual costs of operating the O'Higgins system therefore make it a close call between managing your own Self-Select PEP of £6,000 and trying to choose an Equity Income trust *with a better than average performance*. However, the key point is that your PEPs should grow and once they reach a significant figure the argument for doing it yourself becomes much more persuasive.

HOW TO SELECT SHARES FOR THE SYSTEM

Selecting the shares for any of the O'Higgins methods is very simple and can be fun. Many of the Sunday newspapers show the full list of FT-SE 100 companies every week and give details of the market capitalisation and dividend yield of each share. If you are following the leading companies method, you are only interested in the 30 companies with the largest market capitalisations. The *Sunday Times* and *Independent on Sunday* make this easy for you, as their lists are in order of market capitalisation. The *Observer* and *Sunday Telegraph* lists are in alphabetical order, so to eliminate the 70 smallest companies you need to establish a benchmark figure, such as £4 billion, and put a line through all the companies with capitalisations below it. In June 1994, this would have left about 40 companies with no line through them. The last ten are then easy to eliminate one by one.

Now you have the list of the top 30 UK companies measured by market capitalisation. The next step is to look at the dividend yields and again to choose a benchmark figure, such as 4%, that is obviously insufficient to qualify for the top ten high-yielders among the 30 shares. Put a line through any share yielding below 4% and you will probably be left with about 15 shares. It is then an easy task to eliminate the remaining five lowest-yielders. Now you have the list of the ten highest-yielders out of the top 30 companies. These are the shares you want, if you intend to follow the basic O'Higgins high-yielding system. Over the last ten years, the Johnson Fry research demonstrated that in the UK the ten highest-yielders beat the market by 3.1% per annum.

If you decide instead to opt for O'Higgins' more refined method, you cross off, from the list of highest-yielders, the five with the highest share prices. The remaining five shares are the recommended portfolio for the O'Higgins highest-yield/lowest-price method of investing. This is the system that beat the UK market by 8.1% per annum excluding costs over ten years.

If you prefer the diversity offered by the FT 30 Share Index (as opposed to the extra security of the higher market capitalisations of the top 30 shares), you can do exactly the same exercise using the FT 30 Index. All you need to do is to ask your broker to supply the list of companies in the index together with their market capitalisations, prices and dividend yields.

Johnson Fry found that, using the top 30 shares, the second highest-yielder worked well in the UK. If you want to try this approach for your single company PEP, you should re-examine the list of ten highest-yielders and select the share with the second highest-yield. Over the ten years ending 1993, this system beat the UK market by 10.9% per annum excluding costs.

As you can see, it is a remarkably simple exercise to select a system portfolio or a single share in this way. You do not even have to know anything about the companies in question. Once a year you repeat the whole process, when you will find that a few shares need to be replaced.

JOHNSON FRY'S SCHEME

Inspired by the results of our research, Johnson Fry has developed a scheme for running PEPs for investors based on the O'Higgins approach using the broadly based FT 30 Index. There will be no front-end fee, but there is a 5% penalty for withdrawal in the first year, reducing by 1% per annum thereafter. For investors taking a five-year view, this should therefore cost nothing. Dealing costs will be a very cheap 0.4% per transaction and Johnson Fry will handle all the administration including annual switches, reclaiming the tax on dividends and reinvesting them if required. The annual management charge will be 1.5% plus VAT. If you require further details, Johnson Fry's address and telephone number is 20 Regent Street, London, SW1Y 4PZ (Tel: 0171-321 0220).

SUMMARY

1. Chase de Vere's booklet gives a detailed list of managers for Self-Select PEPs. Each PEP scheme has to be considered on its merits as charges can vary considerably.

2. Self-Select general PEPs can be invested in qualifying unit and investment trusts and shares or any combination of them. There is also a £1,500 allowance for investing in non-qualifying trusts within PEPs.

3. It makes sense to use the £1,500 annual allowance for non-qualifying trusts in PEPs to obtain geographical diversification into high growth areas and/or as a kind of insurance by an investment in gold.

4. If you prefer to manage your own money, you should consider using an execution-only broker to save on initial and management charges and dealing commissions.

5. The O'Higgins approach, *based on the past ten years' results*, seems to offer better than average returns. His methods, adapted for the UK market, include buying:

    a. The ten highest-yielders from the top 30 companies. (This system produced a 22.4% compound annual return against 18.8% for the UK market.)

    b. The five lowest-prices shares from the ten highest-yielders (26.1% against the market's 18.8%.)

    c. The second lowest-priced of the ten highest-yielders. However, in the UK, the second highest-yielder is a more consistent and simpler alternative (29.7% against 18.8%).

    For investors who want the comfort of better diversification (as opposed to the extra security of the higher market capitalisations of the top 30 shares), the FT 30 Share Index is the alternative source for their selections and works just as well.

6. O'Higgins' methods seem to work both in America and the UK for the following reasons:

    a. There is a strong element of contrary thinking in buying high-yielding shares, which tend to beat the market.

    b. Dividends are a major part of overall market returns.

    c. Leading companies are less likely to fail completely.

    d. Lower-priced shares are subject to larger percentage moves.

7. It is easy to select shares using the O'Higgins principle from your Sunday newspaper. The selection process takes no more than an hour and only needs to be reviewed once a year.

8. Johnson Fry, who researched the O'Higgins system for me, has developed a collective scheme for following the O'Higgins system with no front-end charge, cheap dealing commissions and an annual charge of 1.5% per annum, plus VAT. Like investing in unit and investment trusts, this kind of scheme is not so much fun as managing your own money, but it has the great advantage of being hassle-free. Johnson Fry also provides regular valuations, arranges automatic annual switching and reclaims dividends and, if required, reinvests them.

9. *There is no guarantee that O'Higgins' methods and Johnson Fry's research will work as well in the future as they have in the past. Shares can go down as well as up. One of the companies selected could fail or suffer a major setback, which could have a dramatic effect on a small portfolio. There is no such thing as a completely fail-safe system for investing in equities.*

11

STOCKBROKERS

PROSHARE

Before appointing a stockbroker the small investor should consider joining the ProShare Association, which was formed in April 1992. It is committed to providing individual investors with comprehensive, jargon-free information on all matters relating to share ownership and financial planning. ProShare wants to ensure that private investors have access to everything they need to enable them to make sensible and, they hope, profitable investment decisions.

Membership currently costs £30 per annum, for which you receive a monthly newsletter, *The ProShare Bulletin*, and other benefits, including discounted subscriptions to a number of investor services.

Many potential stock market investors have no one to share their ideas with and are put off by the thought that investing can be a lonely business. In October 1993, ProShare launched ProShare Investment Clubs, a service which helps private investors set up and run clubs to make joint investments with friends or colleagues. Membership is £50 per annum, for which members receive a detailed Investment Clubs Manual, a helpline service and other special offers and discounts. Further information on The ProShare Association or on ProShare Investment Clubs can be obtained from ProShare (UK) Ltd., Library Chambers, 13–14 Basinghall Street, London EC2V 5BQ (Tel: 0171-600 0984).

FINDING A STOCKBROKER

Finding the right stockbroker is not an easy task for investors with small portfolios. Many brokers prefer to concentrate their efforts on the institutions and do not want the administrative hassle of dealing with small accounts.

The Association of Private Client Investment Managers and Stockbrokers, 112 Middlesex Street, London E1 7HY (Tel: 0171-247 7080) will supply a free brochure giving details of those brokers who are interested in private clients with funds of £10,000 (in some cases less), and describing the kinds of services on offer.

For active investors there are two main options: execution-only (simply dealing) or a more comprehensive and traditional service. One of the advantages of the O'Higgins method of share selection is that you can use an execution-only broker as you will not need your hand to be held. Execution-only brokers do not give advice, so they are far cheaper.

If you are selecting growth shares or investing in smaller companies, you may welcome some investment advice and recommendations from a traditional stockbroker. You can also arrange to be informed about directors' dealings in any of the shares in your portfolio and to obtain details of important announcements, perhaps with copies of press cuttings. The more active your account, the more help you can expect from your broker.

Needless to say, you have to pay for the extra services provided by a traditional broker. Their commissions range from about 1.65% down to 0.5% and even lower for really major private clients. Usually there are also minimum charges of about £25 which can be particularly onerous on small transactions. For example, on a small purchase of £500-worth of shares, the commission could be as much as 5%.

SHARELINK

In the past, I always thought that execution-only stockbrokers were a false economy, but that was before I visited the largest one, Sharelink, in Birmingham.

In June 1994, for normal Stock Exchange business, Sharelink's minimum charge is £20 per bargain in each company up to £1,333, 1.5% for orders of £1,333 to £2,500, 0.75% on the next £2,500, and only 0.1% on the excess over £5,000. On a £10,000 order its charges added up to £61.25 (0.61%), but on a £20,000 order they dropped to only 0.33%. This is cheap, even by the standards of execution-only brokers, and very cheap indeed when compared with more traditional brokers offering a fuller service.

For PEPs, Sharelink makes no initial charge and its annual charge is 0.75%, plus VAT, payable quarterly in arrears. This is very reasonable for small PEPs; for larger ones Sharelink charges 0.75% on the first £50,000, 0.25% on the next £50,000 and 0.15% on the excess over £100,000. It also arranges the transfer of PEPs from other managers and meets any charges levied by them up to a maximum of £25 plus VAT per plan.

Dealing is by telephone. Sharelink is open seven days a week and commissions on PEP transactions are the same 1.5% up to £2,500 as they are for their normal dealing service. Above £2,500 there is a maximum charge of £37.50, which is a big advantage as the PEPs grow. On a £25,000 bargain, the commission would be only 0.15%, which is much less than I pay and highly competitive by any standards.

To give you an idea of all the other factors involved in Self-Select PEP schemes, I have reproduced for illustration purposes the Sharelink guide to its general and single company PEP charges. These may be revised later in 1994 and are typical of high-quality execution-only brokers.

Full details of brokers and their charges are given in the Chase de Vere booklet. They vary in almost every respect and you need to study the small print carefully. The main points to note with Sharelink's charges and those of other leading execution-only brokers are the initial charge, the annual charge and the dealing commissions (especially the minimum limit). Then you should study the smaller charges for services like dividend collection, withdrawal of funds, transfers to another fund manager, *ad hoc* valuations and the like. For example, Killik and Co. makes no initial or annual charges, but dealing commission is 1.65% with a minimum of £40. There is also a charge of £7.50, plus VAT, for each and every dividend collected. If you have six shares in your Killik PEP and they are all paying interim and final dividends, this would add £90, plus VAT, per annum to the PEP charges. £90 is 1.5% of the £6,000 annual allowance for a general PEP, so it is quite significant. Also, the minimum dealing charge of £40 is heftier than most and the dealing commission of 1.65% is onerous compared with most execution-only brokers. Reyker Securities, for example, only charges 0.9% dealing commission with a minimum charge of £16. However, it has an initial charge of £40, plus VAT, and an annual management charge of 1%, plus VAT, but no dividend collection charges.

You also need to determine whether or not there is a limit on the number of shares that can be held and if a broker's PEP scheme permits you to hold qualifying investment and unit trusts as well as shares. In

SHARELINK'S GUIDE TO ITS PEP CHARGES		
	'GENERAL' PEP	'SINGLE COMPANY' PEP
ADMINISTRATION CHARGES		
Annual Administration Fee**	0.75%*	0.75%*
Income Facility	FREE	FREE
Ad Hoc Funds Withdrawal	£25*	£25*
Transfer from another Plan Manager	FREE	FREE
Transfer to another Plan Manager	£25*	£25*
Closure of Plan	£25*	£25*
Call Payments & Rights Administration	FREE	FREE
INVESTMENT CHARGES		
Dealing Commission on Purchases & Sales ***	1.5%	1.5%
Minimum £20/Maximum £37.50		
Sale of Shares & Reinvestment into a PEP	Sale commission only	Sale commission only
Transfer of Shares from a New Issue	FREE	FREE
Transfer of Shares from Employee Schemes	N/A	FREE
OPTIONAL SERVICES		
Ad Hoc Statement or Valuation	£5* each	£5* each
Annual Company Report & Accounts***	£10* each	£10* each
Attendance at Shareholders' Meetings	£20* each	£20* each

Gross interest is payable on cash balances held within a Premier PEP. The rates payable are shown opposite and refer to increments over the Bank of Scotland's London Deposit account rate. No interest will be paid on cash balances below £50. The rate of interest paid is subject to a maximum equivalent to the Bank of Scotland's base rate less 1%.

CASH BALANCE	INCREMENT ON ACCOUNT RATE
£5,000 plus	5.0% above
£500-£4,999	3.5% above
£50-£499	1% above

* Plus VAT at the prevailing rate.

** The management fee is deducted quarterly in arrears and is based on the portfolio value. There is a minimum charge of £5 applicable to both 'General' and 'Single Company' PEPs. In the case of Index Funds, the fee excludes any annual charge Gartmore Fund Managers Limited will make to the Unit Trust, which is 0.5% for the UK Index Fund and 0.4% for the European Fund.

*** Except Index Funds options, where the investment fee is 4%. Once invested in either or both Index Funds, investors may elect to switch from one Index Fund to another, subject to a minimum investment level of £250, for a fixed commission of £20. Any additional investment into the new Fund at the time of the switch will incur the normal investment fee.

**** Investors in the Index Funds may request a six monthly Progress Report and a full annual fund report free of charge.

most cases, you are also entitled to hold your full allowance of non-qualifying trusts.

Many of the brokers work closely with unit trust or investment trust groups or manage their own. Sharelink, for example, offers a UK and a European Index Tracking Fund operated by Gartmore. In May 1994, there was a special offer with no initial charge and the minimum investment was only £250. Sharelink advises me that the special offer will be repeated in the future.

SHAREFINDER

The main revelation from my visit to Sharelink was the discovery of its new service 'Sharefinder', which covers the leading 650 companies and has three essential features: a weekly performance summary, a weekly buy/sell guide and individual company reports.

The weekly performance summary costs £2.95 a copy and gives details of price-earnings ratios (PERs), NAVs, yields, gearing and relative performance. The buy/sell guides cost £4.95 each and give details of brokers' consensus recommendations for the same 650 shares. These statistics are useful now and then, but the best value for money is Sharelink's report on individual companies for £4.95 each. The report is produced to order, so you can always be sure of the latest information. It has details of how many brokers have recommended the share as a buy, sell or hold. There is also a computerised consensus commentary, which I tested against three shares I know well and found to be remarkably good in picking up the salient points. In addition, the report includes five-year statistics of earnings, dividends, PERs and key financials, together with major shareholdings, charts and all the latest announcements. At £4.95, this is excellent value for someone contemplating a sizeable investment in a leading company.

It is important to note that Sharelink is not in the business of offering investment advice. However, Sharefinder adds a new dimension to its services and is a very attractive halfway house for small investors who are looking for something extra, but do not need a great deal of help. For further information, telephone 021-200 7777.

TRADITIONAL BROKERS

As I have explained, a traditional broker's commission on purchases and sales of stock can range from 1.65% to less than 0.5%, according to the size of the transaction and the importance of the client. If you want your hand held, you should not begrudge your broker a reasonable commission on each transaction, provided he gives you good service. You want a broker who is switched on and really anxious to help you.

Bear in mind that your broker would be unnatural if he were not to some extent commission-orientated. The more you turn over your portfolio, the more commission your broker will earn in the short run. However, there is no need for alarm as most brokers have the long-term interests of their clients at heart and will not try to persuade them to deal simply to earn more commission.

MINIMUM LEVEL OF SERVICE

The problem for many small investors is that they feel they cannot be too demanding because their account is so tiny and unimportant to the broker. However, there is an absolute minimum of information that the private investor, however small, should be able to request. As the account grows, there is a higher level of service that can be progressively demanded. This is the minimum standard you can reasonably expect as a small private investor:

1. Any verbal or written recommendation from your broker should be accompanied by details of the current PER of the share in question, the dividend yield, the NAV per share, the market capitalisation, the past record of earnings growth, the consensus of estimated future growth, the prospective PER, borrowings and your broker's reasons for buying or selling.

2. Any execution should be carried out efficiently, at the price limit mutually agreed with the broker.

3. Subsequently, you should be kept informed of any major new developments, such as directors' share dealings, any announcements made by the company and details of any sharp price movements.

4. Your broker should be able to help you when you ask for a list of shares that meet certain criteria. For example, you might be looking for a high-yielder and want to be advised which of the FT-SE 100 stocks have dividend yields of over 6%, PERs under 15, gearing of less than 25% and future growth estimated at 10% per annum or more.

    Restrict your requests for the fullest information to those

companies in which you are very likely to invest. You do not want to wear your broker's patience too thin with spurious enquiries.

CONCENTRATE ON THE FACTS

I have, in the past, dealt with brokers who ring me up to say, 'English China Clay looks very good. There is a rumour that Hanson is going to bid.' Or, 'Tesco's results are coming out on Wednesday. They will be better than expected. The shares look very cheap.' I hate this kind of share tip. It is worse than useless – a definite drawback to good money management.

When a broker tells me a share looks attractive, I immediately ask for details of the PER, the asset value, the record over the last five years, the growth rate and the consensus of brokers' forecasts. I want facts and try to limit fancy. If you do the same, your broker will quickly get the message that you, too, are one of those strange people who actually wants to concentrate upon the known facts first, second and last.

12

PORTFOLIO MANAGEMENT

You should only invest in the stock market after you have adequate life insurance, money earmarked for illness, old age and, in some cases, school fees. You also need a reserve for unexpected expenditure like major car repairs. The important point about this warning is that any cash you decide to invest should be genuinely *patient* money. The essential characteristic of patient money is that you should not need to withdraw it suddenly. Being forced to sell equity investments at the wrong moment can be a very painful experience.

How much money you need to begin with is debatable. If you can afford £6,000, a general PEP would seem to be a good starting point. The attractions of investing through a PEP may not be immediately obvious – there will be extra costs and all UK investors already have

131

a £5,800 tax-free annual allowance for capital gains. But PEPs can compound in value and their dividend income is also protected from tax. If you use an execution-only broker and a Self-Select PEP, the charges are relatively negligible and you always have to bear in mind that a future Chancellor might abolish PEPs altogether or reduce the allowances substantially. I am therefore very much in favour of making hay while the sun shines and investing as much as possible in PEPs.

I have already shown you how difficult it is to forecast stock market trends. You might well feel that share prices are too high at the moment. A savings plan is the obvious answer if you are buying unit or investment trusts, or a phased programme of investment if you are managing your own money. I usually work on the rough-and-ready principle of investing only half of my money if I feel bearish, keeping the other half in cash. If I feel bullish, I am usually fully invested. When tuning down from full investment to half investment, I always sell my most speculative holdings. This results in the residual half of my portfolio being much sounder.

SPREAD YOUR RISK

Usually, I recommend that a private investor's general portfolio (PEPs are different, as will be shown) should contain about ten to twelve shares. Your first choice is likely to be better than your second, which in turn should be better than your third and far better than your tenth. Take advantage of running a small portfolio – do not handicap yourself, like an institution, by holding a vast number of different securities. Not only would they be impossible to choose without watering down your selection criteria, but they would also be very difficult to monitor effectively.

With a portfolio of ten to twelve shares, you should make it a policy to put no more than 10% of your money in any one. However attractive a particular investment may appear to be, you should always remember that investing in equities involves risk and that things can go wrong. You may suddenly find that your favourite company has infringed an important patent, that the chief executive has decided to leave, or a major new product has encountered unexpected difficulties. If your portfolio is well spread, you will find unexpected setbacks of this nature much easier to handle both psychologically and financially.

RECORD YOUR INVESTMENTS

I recommend that you purchase a small investment ledger to record the details of purchases and sales of your shares held both within and outside your PEP schemes. Make a note of the level of the FT All-Share Index on the days you make the transactions and the monthly RPI figures as these will give you useful benchmarks against which to measure the performance of individual shares.

For shares outside your PEP schemes the detailed record will be a great help when completing your tax return. You should retain all contract notes as proof of transactions, in case there are any queries. Share certificates should be kept in your own safe or at your bank.

RUN PROFITS AND CUT LOSSES

I often read American books like *The Money Masters*, *The New Money Masters*, *Market Wizards*, and *The New Market Wizards*, reviewing the successful techniques of America's greatest investors. They all seem to share two very important characteristics. First, they have a discipline – a system, a method, an approach to investment that, over the years, they hone and refine. Second, they all seem to run their profits and cut their losses.

Most people's natural instinct is to do the opposite – to cling to loss-making shares in the hope that they will recover and to snatch profits for fear that they will disappear. This is a certain recipe for suffering many large losses and never enjoying a substantial profit.

133

The professional's way usually produces the opposite effect – big profits and small losses.

If you buy a growth share, let the profit run while it continues to perform well. Only consider selling if its performance falters. A similar approach should be adopted for investments in unit trusts and investment trust shares.

When buying shares using the O'Higgins system, or an adaptation of it, you only need to review the portfolio once a year. That is the way the system has worked so well in the past, so do not tamper with it. Any system you use should be followed to the letter. If you find that over a period it is not working for you, there is an obvious remedy.

The O'Higgins system runs profits for a year. In 1992, for example, two shares out of the five made over 40% and in 1993 one made 45% and another 67%. Losses were also run for a year but, because of the high yield (contrary thinking) and systematic approach, they were few and far between. In the Johnson Fry research, out of the 50 shares selected from the top 30 over ten years there were only ten losses, including five in the only down year, of which three were worse than the market. During the ten years only four of the losses were significant (25%, 23%, 18% and 17%); all the rest were under 5.5% and most of them far less.

TYPICAL PEP PORTFOLIOS

Some investors will have all of their stock market money invested in their PEPs; others just a small proportion. A PEP scheme, or a number of them, should form a natural and very attractive part of your overall portfolio. With £30,000 to invest, you could have £6,000 in a general PEP, £3,000 in a single company PEP and £21,000 in other investments – 10% of your portfolio in ten different shares with £3,000 invested in each. Three of the investments would be sheltered from tax by the PEPs, but the other seven would be taxed in the normal way. Each year another £9,000-worth of shares could be PEPed until the whole £30,000 portfolio was sheltered from tax.

For your single company PEP you might prefer to choose the second highest-yielder from the top 30 companies, a well-known leading growth company or a small one of which you have special knowledge. In your general PEP you might like the idea of the wider spread given by the ten highest-yielders in the alternative O'Higgins system. Although the high-yielding system offers greater diversity, historically the performance has not been as good as the highest-yield/lowest-priced system. Over the ten years 1984–93, the compound overall annual return of the ten highest-yielders from the top 30 companies was 22.4% compared with 26.1% for the lowest-priced shares. There is another possible snag – if you invest in ten shares in a general PEP, the average transaction will be only £600. With a minimum commission of say £25, you would therefore be paying over 4% dealing commission, compared with 2% on the five-share system. You might be able to negotiate better terms with your broker for the whole package, but otherwise a 2% difference is too large a handicap.

Although five shares do not provide such a wide spread of risk, under the top 30 O'Higgins system they are all very substantial companies capitalised at not less than £5bn. They are therefore relatively safe. Similarly, a unit or investment trust offers a very wide spread indeed. One fund could serve your interests well, but as your PEPs grow, you would no doubt want to widen your investment perspective.

I will now show you some typical examples of the way to use your general and single company annual PEP allowances. In Portfolio 1, I assume that you are using a Self-Select general PEP and a Self-Select single company PEP and that you are following the O'Higgins system. I also assume that the second highest-yielder has a low share price and is one of the five lowest-priced of the ten highest-yielders.

PORTFOLIO 1

General PEP

£1,500 in each of four of the top 30 high-yielders with the lowest share prices

Single company PEP

£3,000 in the second highest-yielder of the top 30 high-yielders

In Portfolio 2, the second highest-yielder has a high share price, so it is not one of the five lowest-priced shares. However, it is still a good proposition for the single company PEP.

PORTFOLIO 2

General PEP

£1,200 in each of five of the top 30 high-yielders with the lowest share prices.

Single company PEP

£3,000 in the second highest-yielder of the top 30 high-yielders.

Portfolio 3 assumes that you also want to invest in a PEPable non-qualifying unit or investment trust covering a region of the world or sector that appeals to you.

PORTFOLIO 3

General PEP

£1,500 in a PEPable non-qualifying investment or unit trust.
£900 in each of five of the top 30 high-yielders with the lowest share prices.

Single company PEP

£3,000 in the second highest-yielder of the top 30 high-yielders.

There is a vast range of other possible portfolios, two of which are set out below.

PORTFOLIO 4

General PEP

£1,500 in a PEPable non-qualifying trust.

£1,500 in a fast-growing share.

£3,000 in an Equity Income unit trust (with an above-average performance).

Single company PEP

£3,000 in the second highest-yielder of the top 30 high-yielders.

PORTFOLIO 5

General PEP

£1,500 in a fast-growing share.

£1,500 in the second highest-yielder.

£1,500 in a PEPable non-qualifying trust.

£1,500 in an Equity Income unit trust (with an above-average performance).

Single company PEP

£3,000 in a share of which you have special knowledge.

As you can see, the permutations are infinite. I am simply trying to give you a feel for the options at your disposal. Investment is very much a matter of temperament. You might be unhappy about investing £3,000 in just one share. There is no compulsion to take out a single company PEP or invest the maximum of £3,000 in it. If that is how you feel, invest less in your single company PEP or simply concentrate on your general PEP.

ADDING TO YOUR PEPS

When adding to your PEPs in subsequent years, deciding how to allocate your portfolio can be a problem. The key point is that you should always look upon your PEP portfolios as a whole when deciding how much to invest in individual shares. To illustrate how to deal with this, imagine a hypothetical example making the following assumptions:

1. The second highest-yielder is not one of the lowest-priced shares in both year one and year two.

2. The single company PEP is used for the second highest-yielder in year one.

3. The general PEP is used for the five lowest-priced of the ten highest-yielders in year one.

4. At the end of year one, the £3,000 in the single company PEP has appreciated to £4,000 and the £6,000 in the general PEP has appreciated to £8,000.

5. At the beginning of year two, you open another single company PEP and add a further £6,000 to your general PEP. As a result, the single company PEPs total £7,000 and the general PEP £14,000.

To construct the second year's portfolio you need to identify the ten highest-yielders and select from them the second highest and the five with the lowest share prices. Ideally you would like to invest an equal amount (£3,500) in each of the six shares (6 x £3,500 = £21,000), but you have £4,000 in one of the single company PEPs, so use that for the second highest-yielder (and sell the first year's share unless it is the same). You can then invest £3,500 in four of the five lowest-priced shares in your general PEP and use the £3,000 in your new single company PEP for the fifth share.

The shares already held in your PEPs from the previous year should be sold, unless they qualify again for inclusion. In that event, it would be necessary to top up each holding to £3,500. As you can see, minor compromises have to be made over the amounts held in your single company and general PEPs, but always remember to look at your PEP portfolios as a whole.

Many investors would prefer to back professionals rather than try to invest themselves. The answer is simple – unit trusts and investment trusts are tailor-made for you. In that event, you should not participate in a Self-Select scheme; instead join a scheme run by one of the more successful management groups. You can still be the main influence in the shape of your PEP portfolio. With a large group you could, for example, insist on its Equity Income trust for the bulk of the money in the general PEP and a non-qualifying trust for the balance of £1,500 in a Japanese fund or one concentrating on gold shares or some other specialised sector that appeals to you.

One of the first rules of investment is to know yourself. Do not make investments or take risks that are going to cause you loss of sleep. Be comfortable with your investment policy – that way you will be less likely to make bad decisions.

MONITORING YOUR INVESTMENTS

Whether you are invested in unit trusts, investment trusts or shares, and whoever is managing the investments, it is essential to monitor the performance. You need to know if your money is growing or shrinking at the same rate as the market as a whole and if it is keeping up with inflation. If you are interested in a particular sector of the market, or a particular type of unit or investment trust, you also want to know how your investments have performed against others in the same sector or peer group.

This sounds a formidable task, but in practice it is very easy. I have already explained to you in the chapters on unit and investment trusts how to monitor your investments in them. Keep an eye on the daily prices through a leading newspaper and check the performance about once a quarter through *Money Management* and the AITC Monthly Information Service – not only against the market as a whole but also against the average for their sector and the best-performing trusts in it.

Whether or not your investments are keeping up with inflation is simply a matter of comparing their performance against the Retail Price Index (RPI). To calculate the percentage change in the RPI from the month in which you purchased an investment, deduct the figure on the month of purchase from the current level, divide the result by the level on the purchase date and multiply by 100. For example, if the RPI had risen from 150 to 165, then 165-150 = 15 and the percentage is: $\frac{15}{150} \times 100 = 10\%$.

Shares managed on the O'Higgins system, or an adaptation of it, do not need checking regularly; you only need to review them once a year. However, you will no doubt be interested in their progress from time to time, so you can always check the prices in your daily newspapers.

TAXATION

If shares are held in a PEP, it is possible to sell them without any tax consequences. This makes it easier to review them more dispassionately without being overshadowed by the threat of a massive tax bill. If you hold a particular share in your own name and in your PEPs, it is more tax-efficient to take significant profits in your PEP scheme.

For shares outside a PEP scheme, another way of reducing your potential capital gains tax liability is to sell some of your shares and immediately buy them back again. The disposal establishes either a gain to take you up to your tax-free limit or a loss to set off against other gains. The technique is called bed-and-breakfasting and can easily be arranged with your broker before the end of each tax year.

RECOMMENDED READING

Your daily, weekly and monthly reading is an important aid to the effective management of your portfolio. *There is a bare minimum that you should read if you are going to choose shares yourself*: the *Financial Times* every day, another good daily, a leading Sunday paper and the *Investors Chronicle* every week.

The *Financial Times* is one of the finest newspapers in the world and an indispensable tool to the active investor. Even if you do not have time to read the FT thoroughly every day, be sure to read the weekend edition, which summarises the week's movements in major markets and contains excellent articles of a more reflective nature.

When you read the FT, pay particular attention to the reviews of both annual and interim results. Nowadays, you need to study the detailed comment on companies to make sure that earnings are all they seem to be and that, from one year to the next, you are comparing like with like.

In addition, news of a more general nature might also concern you. On the front page of the section dealing with companies and markets, the FT always has an index of all the companies mentioned in the paper that day. You can, therefore, always turn quickly to the relevant page to see if there has been some significant news affecting one of your investments. The kind of event that should alarm you is the sudden departure of an excellent chief executive, the expiry of a major patent or a major new competitor entering the industry. Conversely, there might be the good news of a management change for the better, a major new product or a competitor failing and leaving the field wide open. It is important to keep in touch with your investments, as you do not want to be the last person to hear the news.

The *Investors Chronicle* is the only weekly investment magazine and is an essential tool for the active investor. The annual reviews of company results, with their five-year records, are of particular interest and now highlight changes in accounting to facilitate earnings comparisons.

As I mentioned earlier, the *Chase de Vere PEP Guide* and accompanying performance statistics are indispensable for PEP investors. The AITC Monthly Information Service is also excellent value for £15 a quarter and is essential for monitoring the performance of the underlying net value (as well as the share price) of investment trusts. It also goes into great detail on PEPs, savings schemes, discounts or premiums to NAV, the PEP investment status and other highly relevant information.

Money Management is an excellent monthly magazine available from retailers like W.H. Smith and also by subscription. Although it is mainly for professional advisers, there are detailed articles on a wide range of personal finance subjects.

The main attraction is the very detailed review of the performance of unit trusts, investment trusts and insurance funds. Performance in the preceding month is shown, together with the longer term record over ten, five, three and two years and over the last twelve and six months. (£4.50 monthly; Tel: 0181-680 3786).

Money Observer also has a wide range of features on subjects from investment strategy to company profiles and tax tips. There is a comprehensive 'Databank', detailing the performance of all listed shares, unit and investment trusts. (£2.50 monthly; Tel: 0171-278 2332).

Other publications of interest include *Moneywise*, *Planned Savings*, *Investment Trusts* and *What Investment?* However, as a PEP investor, your main concern will be articles on that subject and on unit and investment trusts together with regular detailed performance tables. *Money Management* and *Money Observer* cater for both of these requirements every month.

More experienced investors will also be interested in investment newsletters. There is a host of them, but the two I like most are *Techinvest* and *The Investors Stockmarket Weekly*. The former concentrates on high-technology companies and has an excellent track record for its share recommendations and model portfolios. Its yearly nap selections of six shares have also performed extremely well (so far); using a one-year time frame they could make an attractive package for an adventurous Self-Select PEP. The annual subscription is £129 (£89 for first-time subscribers) and the publisher's address is Techinvest Limited, Mill House, Naas, Co. Kildare, Ireland.

The Investors Stockmarket Weekly is an informative and effective weekly publication which also has an above-average track record of investment recommendations. It tends to concentrate on small- to medium-sized companies. (Annual subscription £82 with £7 discount for direct debit; Tel: 0171-247 4557.)

Another publication that will be of interest to more advanced investors is *The Hambro Company Guide*, which is a financial directory published quarterly. It gives five-year profits and earnings per share figures of UK quoted companies together with brief details of balance sheets, gearing, return on capital employed, activities and key dates. (Annual subscription £99 or £65 for Fidelity customers; Tel: 0171-278 7769.)

The Estimate Directory is also a useful monthly publication giving brokers' estimates of future earnings and establishing a consensus. The annual subscription is £350 but there is also a quarterly subscription for private investors, costing £120 (reduced to £105 if paid by direct debit or credit card). Less active investors should bear in mind that their brokers will almost certainly subscribe to *The Estimate Directory* and should be able to supply details of consensus forecasts. (Tel: 031-220 0468.)

I have recently devised some new financial products in conjunction with Hemmington Scott, the publishers. They will appear under the generic name of *REFS* (Really Essential Financial Statistics); the first one, *Company REFS*, should be available before the end of 1994. *Company REFS* will provide institutional and active private investors with monthly financial statistics and other company details such as prospective PERs and dividend yields, growth rates, price-to-book values, return on capital employed, EPS on an FRS3, IIMR and normalised basis, profit margins on turnover, EPS growth over five years, gearing, sales-to-market capitalisation ratios, tax rates, brokers' consensus forecasts and PEGs. There is also an excellent chart of the relative strength of each share against the market, its relationship to EPS growth, highs and lows over the last few years and the average PER in each year.

In addition, *Company REFS* includes tables showing the best (and in a few cases the worst) shares in terms of dividend yields, relative strength, PERs, EPS growth, prospective EPS growth, return on capital employed, gearing, price-to-book value, price-to-research and development expenditure and contenders for promotion to and demotion from the various indices. The tables are separate for each of the FT-SE, Mid 250 and SmallCap indices and also for shares not yet in any index.

As if all this is not enough, *Company REFS* will also provide a complete list of warrants and convertibles, a detailed schedule of directors' dealings during the last six months, a list of chief executive officer changes, a monthly list of all company profit and dividend announcements and preliminary headline numbers. It will also highlight any revisions of earnings forecasts made during the month. I have dwelt on *Company REFS* at length because it has been a labour of love and the details show you the many factors involved in the professional management of a share portfolio. I believe that *Company REFS* is unique as a single source for the key information needed to make effective investment decisions. *Company REFS* will be available both monthly and quarterly. If you need further particulars, contact Hemmington Scott Publishing, City Innovation Centre, 26 Whiskin Street, London EC1R 0BP (Tel: 0171-278 7769.)

BOOKS TO READ

If you are a complete novice, begin your investment reading gently, as otherwise you could easily become discouraged. As a first step, try *Investment Made Easy*, which covers deposits, gilts, loan stocks, PIBs, unit and investment trusts, life insurance and pensions, property, alternative investment, taxation and financial advisers. It also has a second part on share investments, working up from the language of finance to reading accounts and then to selecting shares.

If, after reading this, you still feel uncertain about the rudiments of investment, I recommend *The Beginner's Guide to Investment* by Bernard Gray and *How to Read the Financial Pages* by Michael Brett. Both of these are good primers.

After you have a broad understanding of stocks and shares, you should, of course, read *Beating the Dow* by Michael O'Higgins with John Downes. My suggestions for managing high-yield portfolios (especially those with low share prices) within PEPs have been based on O'Higgins' thoughts as applied to the UK market. You will obtain a far better understanding of the underlying strategy if you read his classic book.

If you want to progress further, I suggest you try *The Zulu Principle*, which is for more advanced stock market investors. Afterwards, you would enjoy *The Midas Touch* by John Train which gives a detailed exposition on the strategies that have made Warren Buffett America's pre-eminent investor. There is then a long string of books that I describe in some detail in both *Investment Made Easy* and *The Zulu Principle*. In particular, *One up on Wall Street* by Peter Lynch and his second book *Beating the Street* are very good value, and in the UK *Interpreting Company Reports and Accounts* by Geoffrey Holmes and Alan Sugden is a must for serious investors.

The important point to remember is that if you intend to become more knowledgeable about investment, you cannot escape further homework. A few hours a week will suffice. I recommend that, as you progress, you make a written note of any particularly interesting and impressive points made by authors and financial journalists. In this way, you will be able to compile your own handbook of maxims and guidelines to keep you on the straight and narrow path towards successful investment.

13

SOME QUESTIONS ANSWERED

To keep the preceding chapters fast-flowing I deliberately avoided explaining some important caveats and queries, and reiterating a few of the key points. I hope the responses to the following questions will answer any residual doubts you may have.

1. Can a married couple form a PEP in their joint names?

No. PEPs must be in one name and the address given cannot be 'care of' someone else. A man and his wife can each take out £6,000 in general PEPs and £3,000 in single company PEPs, totalling £18,000 every year.

2. *Can you borrow money from your bank or someone else to take up your PEP allowance?*

Peps were introduced to encourage individual share ownership, so the cash to form them must be seen to come from the individual in question. A husband or wife can pay with a cheque from their joint account, but a husband cannot pay for his wife's PEP with one of his cheques, and vice versa.

There is, of course, nothing to stop you borrowing money and using that money to take up your PEP. They key point is that the cash must be seen to come from you. PEPs cannot be used as security for a bank loan. However, Sharelink, for example, has a loan-back scheme that allows investors to borrow up to 50% of the value of their PEP portfolio on preferential terms from the Bank of Scotland. The Sharelink scheme is designed to provide an alternative to having to make an irrevocable withdrawal from a PEP portfolio, when the cash may only be required temporarily.

3. *Can you transfer existing shares into a PEP?*

If you wish to use your PEP allowances by transferring in shares which you already hold, you can 'Bed and PEP' them by selling the shares in the market and then simultaneously repurchasing them in your PEP. Any profit or loss realised by the sale will be subject to capital gains tax. When selling shares into a PEP, you should bear in mind that the PEP must have been opened prior to dealing.

There is an interesting exception to the above rules whereby shares received by way of a new issue application can be transferred in at cost within 42 days of allotment without the need to Bed and PEP. For this purpose you may only use the unused element of your current year PEP allowances. For example, if in the current tax year you have put £2,000 of cash into your General PEP and not yet opened a Single Company PEP, then you can transfer in £7,000 of the new issue at cost

– £4,000 into your general PEP and £3,000 into a new Single Company PEP.

The new issue rule provides an opportunity to boost your PEPs, if you have subscribed to a very successful new issue and received some shares. Wait until the shares are quoted and have risen to a premium to the issue price, and then (within 42 days of allotment) transfer them into your PEP *at cost*. The profit on the shares, in effect, adds to your annual PEP allowance.

A further exception is made for employees who receive shares from an approved SAYE options scheme. They can transfer their shares into a single company PEP within 90 days of the date of exercise. The transfer is limited to £3,000-worth of shares at the date of transfer. Unquoted shares can also be transferred – the only instance when UK unquoted shares can be used in a PEP.

4. *Is there a double charge for unit trust PEPs?*

On the contrary, you can enter many unit trust PEP schemes for a lesser cost than buying units in the normal way. Few of the management groups have waived their initial charges for PEPs or charge much less than usual (for example, 2% instead of 5%). Their reasoning is that PEP investments will tend to be long term, giving rise to more years of annual management charges. To compensate for reducing initial charges some of them have instituted charges for early exit. Long-term investors in a unit trust PEP scheme are therefore better off than conventional unit holders.

5. *Are there any special advantages in PEP schemes for senior citizens?*

Yes. Money in PEP schemes is outside the Inland Revenue's tax net. Senior citizens can claim higher personal allowances, but they start to lose the extra allowance when their income exceeds a certain limit (£14,200 in May 94). Any tax-free income, such as PEP income, does not count towards the limit. Also, retired people are more likely to want an income from their investments – with PEPs this can be tax-free.

6.   *What other formalities are necessary when forming a PEP?*
You must supply your national insurance number, if not with your application then within 12 months, to qualify for the tax benefits. You also have to sign and date the application form as the plan managers need this to satisfy the Inland Revenue.

7.   *Do you receive any kind of certificate for a PEP?*
No. Usually you will not receive any certificate. Instead the PEP management company will send you a statement or letter acknowledging your entry into the plan and will also send you regular valuations and statements. Keep all the documents you receive in a safe place.

8. *How late can you leave the application for a PEP each year?*

The tax year ends on 5 April and many people make the mistake of thinking that they can enter a new PEP scheme within a few days of applying. There are administrative formalities to be satisfied and many management groups have a seven-day cooling-off period during which you can cancel if you change your mind. This means that, to be on the safe side, you should allow at least 14 days before the end of the tax year to form a new PEP.

9. *Can you transfer PEPs from one scheme to another and how do you do this?*

Yes. You can transfer from one scheme to another, but it can be expensive, so do not make a change lightly. Some management companies allow you to switch funds to another sector within their group. However, if you are really dissatisfied with the performance and/or administration, it may be better to select a completely new manager.

To effect the transfer *contact the new plan manager first* and ask him to arrange the transfer, which will take 4–6 weeks to complete. *Do not tell your existing plan manager* that you are transferring your PEP, as otherwise your holdings might be sold inadvertently and you could lose your PEP allowances as a result. *Let the new plan manager handle everything for you.*

There are usually transfer fee charges of £25–50. Also, some unit trust groups make up for reduced initial charges with charges for making an early exit from their PEP schemes.

10. *Can you obtain shareholder perks with shares owned in a PEP scheme?*

Some UK companies allow shareholders in PEP schemes to benefit from the concessions they offer to their shareholders. Others exclude all shares held in nominee names, which is how shares in PEPs have to be held. To be completely sure of the position, you should double-check with the company secretary of the company in question.

11. *Can you keep cash on deposit in a general PEP and, if so, will the interest be free of tax?*

You can keep cash on deposit, and interest received within the PEP will be tax-free. However, if it exceeds £180 per annum and is distributed to you, it becomes taxable.

12. *Do you have to invest money in a single company PEP immediately?*

The cash must be invested within 42 days of receipt by the plan manager and any new investment must be made within 42 days of settlement of the sale of the last investment.

13. *Can you transfer a PEP to someone else?*

No. You could, of course, distribute the proceeds of selling the shares in the PEP to yourself and give the money to A. N. Other, who could then form a PEP if he or she was over 18, UK resident for tax purposes and had not already used up his or her PEP allowances for the tax year.

14. *Are there any exceptions to the rule that all subscribers to PEPs must be UK residents over the age of 18?*

All subscribers must be over 18, but there is one exception to the UK residents rule – employees of the Crown who are overseas, performing duties as Crown Servants, which are treated for tax purposes as performed in the UK (typically armed forces and diplomats).

15. *What happens if an investor in a PEP becomes non-resident?*

The plan will continue to be exempt from UK tax, but no further subscriptions will be permitted until the investor qualifies again.

16. *Can any quoted EU ordinary shares and/or unit and investment trusts be held within a general PEP scheme?*

Not always. A few plan managers put restrictions on the shares and unit and investment trusts that can be held. Some also limit the number of shares and unit or investment trusts.

17. *Can an investor have one plan manager for a single company PEP and another for a general PEP?*

Yes. You can have as many managers as you have PEPs. In practice, it is easier administratively to use one management group, unless there are very good reasons for using two or more. You can always switch some of your PEPs from one manager to another, but you cannot open more than one single company PEP and one general PEP each year.

18. *Is a PEP mortgage better than an endowment mortgage?*

Endowment mortgages can offer a tax advantage to higher-rate taxpayers, but for everyone else there is no logical reason to mix investment with insurance. Investment through a PEP in unit trusts, investment trusts or shares is cheaper, more flexible and far more tax-effective. Remember though, with a PEP mortgage you need to take out basic life insurance so that the loan will be repaid if you die prematurely.

19. *Do share-exchange schemes offered by some unit trust groups really save money?*

Not always. With some the unit trust manager simply sells your shares and charges normal commission rates, which may not be the cheapest available. James Capel's scheme looks good value; they will sell any one marketable holding of up to £5,000 for up to £10. Save and Prosper will pay the offer price for shares worth £2,500 or more, if it wants them in one of its portfolios. They sell the shares they do not want at bid price and you have to pay brokerage, unless the total value of the shares is £5,000 or more. As you can see, each scheme has to be considered on its individual merits.

20. *What happens if you start a monthly savings plan but cannot keep up the monthly commitment?*

Monthly minimum payments can be as low as £20 but a regular payment commitment by direct debit is usually required. Otherwise, minimum lump sum investments start at around £250. In practice, most managers will not cause a fuss if you were to stop payments. They would probably also allow you to resume them at a later date. But this is a point to be clarified with the plan manager before you commit yourself.

21. *What happens when a PEP investor dies?*

The tax benefits of a PEP belong only to the individual plan-holder and they cease when he or she dies. The investments then form part of the deceased's estate in the normal way.

22. *Do you have to put details of PEPs on tax returns?*

No, because they are completely tax-free. This makes filling in the tax return easier. The only exception is when interest of more than £180 is paid out of the PEP (see question 11). Older people, who can claim higher tax allowances subject to their total income, can ignore any income arising within a PEP.

23. *The rule is that up to £1,500 can be invested initially in a non-qualifying trust, but what happens in later years?*

Let us assume that you invested, through a general PEP plan, the annual allowance of £1,500 in a PEPable non-qualifying unit trust and £4,500 in qualifying trusts. If the £1,500 appreciated to say £10,000 and the £4,500 rose to the same amount, at that point your non-qualifying trusts would be worth 50% of the whole general PEP portfolio. This would be permissible, until you sold the non-qualifying trusts. If you did so and came to reinvest, you would then only be allowed to buy £5,000 (25% of £20,000) worth of other PEPable non-qualifying trusts in the general PEP plan.

On an ongoing basis, you can always reinvest 25% of your general PEP portfolio in PEPable non-qualifying trusts. The only exception to this rule is if, in the first instance, you had used *only* your non-qualifying allowance. In that event, if the £1,500 investment had appreciated to £10,000, you would be able to sell the trust shares or units and reinvest the whole of the proceeds in other non-qualifying trusts.

24. *What is meant by financial commentators when they say a fund is 'fully qualifying' or 'PEPable'?*

To comply with Inland Revenue rules, a unit or investment trust must have at least 50% of its portfolio invested in EU shares (including the UK) to be qualifying or PEPable.

In 1993, two investment management groups ran into problems with the Inland Revenue when they tried to market some trusts as PEPable, despite having less than the required 50% invested in shares. The Revenue ruled that the funds could not even be classified as part of the £1,500 limit for non-qualifying funds; only trusts with at least 50% in *shares* are eligible.

The result of this ruling is that a PEPable fund is more flexible than an individual, as it can invest tax-free just under 50% in gilts and bonds. On the other hand, an individual with a Self-Select general PEP can hold 100% in cash while waiting for a suitable investment opportunity. However, it would be unwise to press this advantage too far, as if no investments were made over a long period there is just a possibility that the Revenue might challenge the PEP plan.

25. *Can you think of any ways of improving PEPs?*

I thought you would never ask. In researching and writing about them, I have developed a few ideas:

1. General and single company PEPs should be merged into one annual PEP allowance. Allowing for inflation, my more generous approach and a liking for round numbers, I would increase the overall limit to £10,000.

2. There is an argument for abolishing the distinction between non-qualifying and qualifying trusts and making it possible to invest PEP funds in any unit or investment trust. However, I can see that the Government will still want to encourage domestic and EU equity investment. Allowing for this, I would increase the initial annual allowance for non-qualifying trusts to a maximum of £2,500 – 25% of my new £10,000 limit. (Under the present rules it is 25% of the £6,000 general PEP limit.)

3. Something needs to be done to make gilts more attractive, so I would allow PEP investors to invest in gilts within the same £2,500 allowance for non-qualifying trusts. The whole of the £10,000 overall limit could be used for EU shares and

qualifying trusts but, if preferred, up to a quarter of it could be invested in gilts and/or non-qualifying trusts.

4. The tax law on dividends should be amended so that they can be paid gross into a PEP scheme, thereby saving a lot of hassle in reclaiming tax and speeding up the whole process.

5. Investors should be allowed to manage their own PEP schemes if they want to do so. I cannot see why active private investors need an approved professional manager for their Self-Select PEPs.

14

SUMMARY

I hope you don't mind me bringing along two advisers

The title of this book sums up my intention – to show you how to *PEP Up Your Wealth*. I hope I have convinced you about a number of ideas that could form the basis of a simple and effective investment strategy. Let me summarise the main conclusions:

1. During the last 75 years, the stock market has been far and away the best medium for investment compared with other financial assets. There is no guarantee that this will continue but, long term, the stock market is likely to remain a relatively attractive proposition.

2. If you can afford it, you should take full advantage of your annual general PEP allowance of £6,000 and your single company PEP

allowance of £3,000. If you can only manage to invest in one, a general PEP scheme is preferable as it is more flexible and more diversified. There is always a possibility that this Government, or a future one, will change the law on PEPs, so make hay while the sun shines.

3. High-yielding shares and trusts have beaten the market on average over the last two decades. Although there is no guarantee that this will continue, there are logical reasons why they have performed so well:

   a. Investing in high-yielding shares contains a strong element of contrary thinking. The market always overreacts both ways – greed pushes shares too high and fear drives them too low. By investing in high-yielding shares you go against the instincts of the herd and buy shares which contain little or no froth.

   b. Dividends are a substantial element of overall stock market returns and by far the most reliable part.

4. Provided you can spare the income, you should reinvest dividends within your PEP. On a cumulative and compounding basis, they make a tremendous difference to long-term overall returns.

5. You should use a savings plan, or invest on a regular basis, to lessen the risk of entering the market with all your funds at just the wrong moment.

6. Unit and investment trusts offer a hassle-free method of investing PEP funds. They also spread risk.

   Over the last decade, the average unit trust has not beaten the market. However, Equity Income unit trusts, which invest in high-yielding shares, have on average matched the market even after allowing for all costs. When selecting Equity Income funds, also consider the best performing Income Growth and High Income investment trusts, which concentrate on high-yielding shares.

7. The points to consider when choosing a suitable unit or investment trust are:

    a. The long term performance – look for consistency.

    b. The recent performance – make sure that the management has not lost its touch.

    c. The performance of the management group's other trusts – ensure that the High Income trust is not a one-off in an otherwise undistinguished stable.

    d. The level of charges – check that they are not excessive. Although charges are not the most important consideration, if too high they can erode performance.

    The *Chase de Vere PEP Guide* is excellent for choosing PEPable unit trusts. The AITC Monthly Information Service is better for investment trusts as it measures the performance of the underlying net assets as well as the performance of the share price.

8. Bear in mind that with an investment trust the discount to net assets and the number of warrants in issue are important investment considerations. The better the performance, the nearer to net asset value you should be prepared to pay, *but always avoid paying a premium.*

9. Record your investments and monitor your performance against the market (measured by the FTA All-Share Index) and inflation (measured by the RPI). The performance of your unit and investment trusts can be monitored by checking the prices in most daily newspapers. For a serious review, use *Money Management*

or a special supplement in the *Investors Chronicle*. To monitor investment trusts the AITC Monthly Information Service is ideal.

10. Consider using the £1,500 annual allowance (out of your general PEP allowance of £6,000) for investing in PEPable non-qualifying unit or investment trusts which focus on areas such as Japan or concentrate on special sectors such as gold.

11. There are three main ways to invest in PEPs other than through unit and investment trusts:

    1. Managed PEP schemes in which you hand over the management to a professional. You can agree in advance on the broad policy to be adopted or, if you prefer, after explaining your objectives, simply hand everything over to the management.

    2. An Advisory PEP in which a broker helps you select shares and unit or investment trusts for your PEP schemes.

    3. A Self-Select PEP in which you select the shares and/or trusts yourself (in some cases with help from brokers on a more informal basis than with an Advisory PEP).

12. If you decide upon a Self-Select PEP, consider the O'Higgins method of investment for selecting shares for both your general and single company PEPs. *On the basis of past results*, over the last two decades, the O'Higgins system has beaten the market by a wide margin. In particular, the five shares with the lowest price out of the ten highest-yielders in either the FT 30 or the top 30 companies, seem tailor-made for a general PEP. The second highest-yielder has also been a consistent and excellent performer and appears to be an attractive way of selecting a share for a single company PEP.

13. The O'Higgins system has worked well because it also concentrates on high-yielding shares which tend to beat the market for the reasons stated in point 3. The additional advantages of the O'Higgins approach are that leading companies are less likely to fail completely and lower-priced shares are subject to larger percentage moves.

14. If you use the O'Higgins system, it will pay you to appoint an execution-only broker for both the administration of your PEP scheme and dealing in the shares within it. The savings of commission are considerable when compared with traditional brokers, who offer advice on share selection. If you prefer to have someone operate the O'Higgins system for you, the Johnson Fry scheme is a relatively inexpensive and effective way of arranging this.

15. You will notice that I have stressed that the O'Higgins system has only worked *on the basis of past results*. The last 20 years and, in particular, the last ten have been very good periods for share-ownership. Shares can go down as well as up. In spite of the relative safety of the top 30 and FT 30 Share Index shares, one of them might fail. No system of share investment is infallible. Indeed, in the unlikely event that a system appeared to be infallible for any length of time, it would soon become self-defeating as more and more investors poured their money into it.

As you can see, PEPs are central to many of the above ideas and PEP schemes are an essential ingredient of any well-planned portfolio. The Conservative Government and, in particular, Lord Lawson, should be congratulated for introducing them. They are a wonderful incentive to save and they also encourage wider share ownership.

When anything is as attractive as PEPs, one always wonders if it will last, There is an obvious risk that the present Government, or a future one, will change the rules in a material way or abolish PEPs altogether. However, PEPs are very popular indeed, so any government will tread very warily when dealing with them. The most likely future development would be further tinkering with the benefits of PEPs by, for example, lowering again the ACT deduction from dividends.

Any change is unlikely to be retrospective and, meanwhile, PEPs offer a simple way of enhancing the returns you enjoy on your investments by saving all taxes. They provide a perfect way of building a significant and flexible tax-free pool of money that can be used for overcoming many of life's financial hurdles.

If you are not already making use of your PEP allowances, you should give serious consideration to getting started. The Chinese have a saying 'A long march begins with a single step' – as a first one buy the Chase de Vere guide, which only costs £9.95. Also, buy the occasional issue of *Money Management* and the *Investors Chronicle* and read the City pages of your daily newspapers (especially the

Sundays) and at least the Saturday edition of the *Financial Times*. In particular, study the leading articles on investment and on the evolving market in PEPs.

When you feel ready, appoint a stockbroker and seek advice until you feel confident enough to manage your own portfolio. Investment is like so many other activities – the more you concentrate on it, the more successful you are likely to be. As you progress, you will want to take the *Investors Chronicle* every week and to read some books on investment. The degree of expertise you achieve is directly dependent upon your own efforts. It is entirely up to you.

Whatever else you decide, remember that your annual PEP allowances vanish if you do not use them before the end of each tax year. They are an incredibly attractive gift from the Government, so, if you can possibly afford to do so, take full advantage of them.

APPENDIX

Johnson Fry has supplied the following notes on its methods and sources for checking the application of Michael O'Higgins' methods to UK stocks.

A UK portfolio of five stocks is selected by applying the criteria used by O'Higgins in America. First, the ten highest-yielders are taken from the 30 companies with the largest market capitalisations in the FT-SE 100. Then the five with the lowest share prices are selected. The strategy is simply to buy the five-share portfolio and hold it for one year, at the end of which the stocks are sold. All proceeds from the sale of the shares *plus the gross dividends received* during the year are then used to purchase five new shares, which are again selected using the O'Higgins method. This process is repeated annually on each anniversary date.

In all the calculations, Johnson Fry has assumed that *gross* dividends are not reinvested when paid, but at the end of the year during which the selected stocks were held. It has also been assumed that no interest is earned on dividend cash payments while awaiting reinvestment and ACT is reclaimed in time for reinvestment at the anniversary date.

Performance comparisons of portfolios constructed using the O'Higgins method have all been made using total returns. The definition of the annual total return of any portfolio, with dividends reinvested annually, is the sum of the capital return, which is the price gain or loss, plus all dividend payments and tax reclaimed. This total cash gain for the year is then expressed as a percentage of the original purchase price of the portfolio to provide the total return.

All calculations were based on data supplied by Datastream. Adjusted stock prices and dividend yields that take account of capital reorganisations were used to calculate price gains and losses at the close of the last trading day for each calendar year and to identify the shares with the highest yield. Historic unadjusted prices were used to select the lowest-priced shares.

The dividend yield provided by Datastream is the latest annualised rate and is defined as the sum of the latest two half yearly or four quarterly gross dividend payments. Although an extensive history of dividend yields for individual stocks is provided, only a limited history of the actual cash dividends paid is available.

In order to calculate the historic total returns of the portfolios, it was necessary therefore to devise a method for estimating the annual cash dividend payments, which, prior to 1988, are not available in Datastream. The method used to estimate the annual cash dividend paid on a specific share was to multiply the Datastream annualised dividend yield for that share at the end of the holding period by the share price at the end of that same period. This estimated annual dividend cash payment was then expressed as a percentage of the share price at the beginning of the period, thereby providing the required estimate of the dividend component of the total return. By adding this yield to the percentage capital gain or loss for the one-year period, an estimate of the total return was obtained. Cumulative total returns for any periods longer than one year were then developed by compounding these annual total returns.

If a stock was acquired or merged into another, it was sold at the date of change and the total return to that point was used as the total return for the entire year.

Datastream's total return index for the All-Share is used for all performance comparisons. This index is based upon adjusted prices and yields and assumes that gross dividends are reinvested when paid.

INDEX